*Given to*

_____

*on the* _____ *day of* _____

*from*

_____

# THE GIFT
## *of*
# FAMILY

# Acknowledgments

"No man is an island unto himself."

My loving thanks to:

my parents, who instilled in me the value, love, and commitment to family;

Jim, the best husband and dad imaginable, who loves and supports me through each challenge;

our children, Mark, Beth, and Katherine for being willing recipients of our attempts at creating a healthy family;

Michael Clifford, who introduced me to Ron Haynes and Thomas Nelson Publishers;

and a special thanks and tribute to Georglyn Rosenfeld, whose research, counsel, creativity, and wealth of publishing knowledge guided me in the scripting of my heart message.

# THE GIFT
## *of*
# FAMILY

*A Legacy of Love*

NAOMI RHODE

THOMAS NELSON PUBLISHERS
NASHVILLE

. . . . . . . . . . . . . . . . . . . . . . .

# OTHER BOOKS BY THE AUTHOR

*More Beautiful Than Diamonds*

4th Reprint: Oct. 1997

Published in Nashville, Tennessee, by Thomas Nelson,
Inc.

Printed in the United States of America.

Scripture quotations are from the NEW KING JAMES
VERSION of the Bible. Copyright © 1979, 1980, 1982,
Thomas Nelson Publishers, Inc.

**Library of Congress Cataloging-in-Publication Data**

Rhode, Naomi.
    The gift of family : a legacy of love / Naomi
Rhode.
        p.   cm.
    ISBN 0-8407-7458-3 (hc)
    1. Family.  2. Parenting.  I. Title.
HQ518.R46   1991
    306.85—dc20                         90-28466
                                           CIP

Printed in the United States of America
4 5 6 7 8 9 BVG 01 00 99 98 97

# Contents

# PART ONE

# *A*
# *Legacy*
# *of*
# *Love*

. . . . . . . . . . . . . . . . . .

# • *What Is a Family?* •

The happiest moments of my life have been
the few which I have passed at home
in the bosom of my family.
THOMAS JEFFERSON

*T*his book is for all families and about all families, regardless of their condition. My desire is to help you to improve the quality of your family life, to help you strengthen the bonds between your family members. I write it out of a deep love and passion for the purpose of family!

We all have our own version of the perfect family. Your concept may be similar to or totally different from mine. But regardless of the family you want or have, your family and my family meet similar needs. They create a bridge between loneliness and love, isolation and companionship, grief and comfort. And they can carry us from darkness into light, from despair into hope, from sorrow into happiness.

Some people claim the family is an endangered species. The family is not dying, but it is changing and adapting. According to Margaret Mead, "No matter how many communes anybody invents, the family always creeps back." Not surprising, as the family was created and ordained by God.

Family relationships involve complex patterns of companionship that don't always involve sharing the same house or the same bloodlines. Living arrangements are as diverse as families. The important thing is to feel like a family and act like a family. A real family has an attitude of concern and tender, loving care for each of its members, regardless of kinship.

What is the perfect family for you? I can't describe it but I can tell you something about it. I believe the closest you will ever come to having a perfect family is the family you have right now. If you didn't make the right choices in the past, work to make your choices right in the present. Remodeling is a lot easier than building anew. You might fantasize about how much better your family would be if you had a different spouse or a different set of circumstances, but that only prevents you from appreciating the value of what you have right now. A new situation might eliminate some of your current problems, but it also presents new problems, complicated by the pain of the disposal of the old.

My husband, Jim, and I have been richly blessed through our family, and I will share with you the guidelines we've followed. We believe the adage that *"The best thing a father can do for the emotional health and strength of his children is to love their mother."* It's not a blueprint that guarantees success, but it has worked for us. Two builders can use the same plans and have the final results turn out quite differently, depending upon the materials used, the foundation and the soil it is built on, the weather, the workers and their commitment to excellence, and other unforeseen factors.

Don't compare your family relationships to ours or to others and devalue what you have. Often the family tree spreads its roots deeper into the soil and grows into an unusual shape. Enjoy your family regardless of the shape of your family tree. Use some of the principles in this book to revitalize your family, find enjoyment in it, and increase your love for each other.

Your family is a gift, a source of pleasure, concern, and emotional support. You may not have a "perfect" family, but you can have a happy family. Love comes in every shape and style.

> Call it a clan, call it a network, call it a tribe, call it a family. Whatever you call it, whoever you are, you need one.
>
> JANE HOWARD

# • A Legacy of Love •

The only thing of value we can give kids is
what we are, not what we have.
LEO BUSCAGLIA

*A*llow me to introduce you to my family. You're going to
be hearing about them in this book, so introductions are important. Jim (the greatest husband in the world) and I have
been married for over thirty years, and we have three wonderful children, Mark, Beth, and Katherine. Each of our children married, and each new spouse brought into our family a
wonderful legacy of love. Each new family opened a new
world of interests and opportunities, while sharing the same
values and ideals which we hold dear. They changed their
lives as well as ours when they brought another family into our
extended family relationships.

Mark married Melody and also became a member of the
Goddard family. Melody's father had been a pastor and a pro-
fessor at Fuller Theological Seminary for years, and her sister
Mary is a missionary in Paris. As Mark's life became merged
into their lives, he also became active in the organizations in
which the Goddard family was involved.

Beth married Curt and was initiated into the Hamman family of four sons. They love scuba diving and collecting rare
shells. Beth soon became a certified scuba diver, and influ-
enced Katherine and Mark to also become certified scuba
divers, something our family had never done. Medical missionary work in Honduras and Mexico was also a part of the
Hamman family, so Beth became involved using her skills as
a dentist.

Our youngest daughter, Katherine, married Ken Magnu-
son (who is also one of four sons) and moved to Minnesota
where Ken's father, grandfather, and great-grandfather have
all been professors at Bethel Seminary, and his oldest brother,
Doug, is a missionary. Katherine has joined in with Ken's
family's love of ministry and sports.

Our family businesses are Semantodontics and Smart
Practice, which serve the dental and medical professions. All

three kids and their spouses have worked for our company at one time or another. Mark and Curt are currently vice presidents—Mark, with education and experience in marketing, and Curt, as a physician.

Why are these factors important in the lives of our children? Because it is a part of their identity, their roots, their sense of belonging. When our kids married, they didn't just marry a spouse—they married into a family. When they became engaged, they realized they would pass the family heritage of their partner on to their children and grandchildren, and they began to discover the rich background of each family.

I love the story a second grade teacher in Cincinnati, Ohio, shared. At the beginning of the school year she asked each of her students to stand up, give their name, and tell a little about themselves. Proud of her rich heritage, one little girl stood up and said: "My name is Martha Bowers Taft. My great-grandfather was president of the United States. My grandfather was a United States senator, and my daddy is ambassador to Ireland." Smiling broadly she then announced, "And I am a Brownie Scout."

Not only did Martha Bowers Taft have an impressive legacy, but Jonathan Edwards and his wife Sarah also left a very impressive legacy. Among their fourteen hundred descendants there were thirteen college presidents, sixty-five college professors, one hundred attorneys, thirty judges, sixty-six physicians, and eighty holders of public office which included three senators, three governors, and a vice president of the United States.

What kind of legacy are you leaving to your family? We can't all leave a prestigious background or lots of money to our children, but we can leave them a legacy of love. A legacy of strength, integrity, caring, and sharing. A legacy of memories of spending lots of time together. A legacy of taking a special interest in the children's lives and activities. A legacy of commitment to them and involvement in their lives. Most importantly, a legacy of spiritual heritage which can be passed on to future generations.

Abraham Lincoln once said, "I don't know who my grandfather was, but I am much more concerned to know who his grandson will be." Who you are and the family you build will be the legacy you will give your children.

# • *God Planned a Family* •

$\mathcal{S}$ince before any of us were born, God planned for us to share our lives with each other. He knew exactly how our strengths and weaknesses would balance one another and the depth of love, understanding, and commitment we would learn to feel.

He knew that the richness of our separate characters would be developed through the hard times and that mutual trust and respect would be born as a result of overcoming the trials together.

He knew that we would laugh together and cry together. He knew we needed each other . . . to hug, to help, to teach, to serve . . . to love.                                  G. COPELAND

# • *What Is a Healthy Family?* •

$\mathcal{T}$o parents, it often appears that professionals in the various institutions of our lives—school, court, church, health, government, sports—have different, often self-serving definitions of the healthy family.

Police officers identify a healthy family by its absence of criminal activity. Teachers define it by school attendance and the willingness of parents to support educational goals. Church leaders look for faithful attendance at services and weekly support envelopes. Doctors and public health officials require the absence of major physical and mental health problems. Coaches pronounce a family healthy if it volunteers eagerly and never misses a game. All these criteria present parents with a plethora of confusing standards.

DOLORES CURRAN

## • *The Threads That Hold Us Together* •

*A* family is a mobile strung together with invisible threads—delicate, easily broken at first, growing stronger through the years, in danger of being worn thin at times, but strengthened again with special care. A family—blended, balanced, growing, changing, never static, moving with a breath of wind—babies, children, young people, mothers, fathers, grandparents, aunts, uncles—held in a balanced framework by the invisible threads of love, memories, trust, loyalty, compassion, kindness, in honor preferring each other, depending on each other, looking to each other for help, giving each other help, picking each other up, suffering long with each other's faults, understanding each other more and more, hoping all things, enduring all things, never failing! Continuity! Thin, invisible threads turning into thin, invisible metal which holds great weights but gives freedom of movement—a family! Knowing always that if a thread wears thin and sags, there is help to be had from the Expert—the Father—"Of whom the whole family in heaven and earth is named."

EDITH SCHAEFFER

. . . . . . . . . . . . . . . . . .

# PART TWO

# *Building with Honor*

. . . . . . . . . . . . . . . . . .

# • *Developing a Sense of Purpose* •

What our deepest self craves is not more enjoyment, but
some supreme purpose that will give unity and
direction to our life. We can never know the
profoundest joy without a conviction that our life
is significant—not a meaningless episode.
KENNY J. GOLDRING

*P*urpose is a driving force that gives meaning to life and
helps individuals grow and develop talents and abilities that
might otherwise lay dormant. You and I may not have any
desire to be world famous, but we can do something that no
one has ever done before. We can build a family like no other
in the world. A family that reaches out with love, acceptance,
and patience to each member and all those who come in contact with it. A family that encourages each member to grow,
develop their God-given talents and abilities, and fulfill his or
her own particular destiny.

Every family and every individual in it needs to identify its
purpose in order for that family to have unity and direction.

Your purpose as a family determines where you live, how
you spend your money and your time, your values, and your
priorities. The quality of your family life, your relationships
with each other, your extended family, and your fellow man
are all directly related to your purpose.

Without a specific purpose in mind, the family might end
up a separate group that does not form a cohesive whole. Your
behavior and activities are going to be based upon your values, whether or not you identify your purpose.

Our family values are built around our belief in God, marriage, each other, time together, education, travel, friendships, service, and experiences more than possessions.

What we wanted as a family has guided our life decisions.
When our children were very young, Jim's and my salaries
were the equivalent of a schoolteacher's salary. We asked our
children whether or not they would like to move out of our
relatively small tract home to a larger home or spend a portion
of every summer in Hawaii. They chose Hawaii . . . a decision

that shaped their lives. With only a moderate income but with our family's values and purpose, we made choices that allowed us to travel and experience life to a far greater extent than if we had lived in a larger home with more material possessions than many of our friends valued.

Building a strong family takes considerable planning, patience, and expertise, as well as generous doses of love, tolerance, and forgiveness.

The Rhode family has endeavored to build on a strong foundation, a foundation of:

- commitment to each other, our family, and our beliefs
- acceptance and affirmation of each family member
- spiritual beliefs which sustain us and our children
- mentors to show our kids the way
- love, which is our safety net

We all have a choice about the methods we use to build our family, methods which are conventional or unorthodox. But regardless of the methods, we will always reap the consequences of our choices. Challenging and frightening, isn't it?

Purpose. Values. Choices. Each of these determines the outcome and shape of your family as they did ours. I challenge you to select a purpose for your family as you read this book. Identify your family values. Make the right choices. Use your energies, material wealth, and ingenuity to build a family of significance, so they can then pass those same values and purposes on to the next generation as a legacy of love.

> To build a family on the love of God is the greatest thing any man can do.
> ROSEY GREER

# • *Choosing Who We Are* •

Parents must be consistently truthful. You can't run games
on kids. You must be honest with them and tell
them the truth and let the truth stand.
ROSEY GREER

"*B*ecause you are our very cherished daughter, I made a
special gift for you," my father told me during his presentation ceremony the night before I left home to go to camp for
the first time. "I want you to accept this gift as a very special
sign of our love. *When you look at it, remember who you are.*"

Even though I was only twelve, I knew that in our family
"remembering who you are" meant we were children of wonderful people with great ancestors of deep spiritual faith.

After his speech of affirmation, my dad presented me with
a piece of wood he had carved and painted into the shape of an
animal that resembled a penguin. He named the carving,
Goofus.

The next day I went to camp with Goofus in my suitcase as
a reminder that I was a special person. Raised in an atmosphere of high trust and low fear, I was assured of my parents'
confidence in me to make good choices.

While at camp I met a fourteen-year-old boy with whom I
became so enraptured that I gave him Goofus. As an adult I
don't understand that choice, but as a child it made perfect
sense.

"Dad, I gave Goofus away to the boy I am going to marry,"
I proudly explained when I got home.

Dad's response was classic: "He must be a very special
person."

Rather than degrading, disciplining, or reprimanding his
twelve-year-old daughter for thinking so little of his gift, he
accepted my choice. Unfortunately Dad died a year later, so
he didn't live long enough to experience the reality of his
statement. The boy's name was Jim Rhode, and seven years
later I married him. We kept Goofus as a reminder of my
dad's confidence in my ability to make the right choices.

Though I'm not saying that any twelve-year-old is capable

of making a decision about marriage, my dad's attitude toward me was important. While raising my own children, I frequently thought of Goofus and the confidence my dad always had in me, as I trusted and affirmed my children's decisions.

As parents we don't always approve of our children's choices, but how should we respond to them? We can affirm their choices; help them live with the consequences; show them love and kindness; affirm their personhood; be compassionate; hold them accountable for carrying them out; or intervene, correct, or prohibit when necessary.

As a rule, we allowed our children to make their own choices within the limits of their maturity, and then to live with the consequences. However, if we felt their choice endangered them mentally, emotionally, physically, or spiritually (which was very seldom), we stepped in and honestly expressed our reservations. What a thrill to have them respect us enough to hear our concerns and act on them as they moved toward independence.

# • *The Best Choice* •

*H*e knows, He loves, He cares,
Nothing this truth can dim,
He gives the very best to those
Who leave the choice with Him.

# • *The Sculptor* •

*I* took a piece of plastic clay
And idly fashioned it one day,
And as my fingers pressed it, still
It bent and yielded to my will.

I came again, when days were passed,
The bit of clay was hard at last,
The form I gave it, still it bore,
But I could change that form no more.

Then I took a piece of living clay
And gently formed it, day by day,
And molded with my power and art,
A young child's soft and yielding heart.

I came again when years were gone,
No longer a child I looked upon.
But still that early impress bore,
And I could change it, nevermore.

UNKNOWN

Always remember that what happens around us is largely
outside our control, but the way we choose to react to it is
inside our control.                    UNKNOWN

# • *Freedom of Choice* •

Love is not a feeling but a choice.
KIERKEGAARD

*A* few years ago, Jim and I traveled to China to conduct a seminar. All of us gained a renewed appreciation for the freedom of choice we have in America, a freedom we often take for granted here.

While in Shanghai we spoke with a young man in a shop. "What do you like best about China?" he asked.

"It's hard to decide between the Great Wall and the terracotta warriors," I responded.

"How I would love to see them," he said wistfully.

"You haven't seen them?" I asked.

"No, when I was eighteen I was assigned to this job behind this counter in this department of this store. I will stay here the rest of my life. You have to have permission to leave Shanghai, and I doubt that I will ever earn it."

After being in China two weeks, I realized the government was making most of the choices for the people, choices as minor as what colors to wear and as major as where to work and the number of children to have. Only one child per family was allowed, which means there are no cousins, aunts, or uncles in the extended families.

We heard rumors that if a little girl is born first, especially in rural areas, she may mysteriously disappear. They don't place much value on the lives of little girls.

Our bus stopped for a thirty-minute break at the Bund, an area near the river where the intellectuals come during lunch, hoping to meet Americans and to practice their English. The weather was very, very cold, and despite the many layers of clothes I wore to keep warm, I was still freezing and didn't want to get off the bus.

"Nothing happens on the bus, Naomi," Jim said, as he went outside.

Realizing I might miss something, I left the semi-comfort of the bus for the blistering wind and cold.

A very atypical Chinese lady rushed up to me and said, "How long are you going to be here?"

"About a half hour," I replied.

"Will you just talk to me? Tell me everything about America."

What would you have said? How would you explain America—*all* about America—in one half hour?

I told her about choices in America, the choices that our one family has made and the consequences of those choices. I took out a family picture, introduced her to each one of our children, and explained the choices we had made as a family unit. Choosing each other as marriage partners, choosing to have three children, choosing to leave the East and move to Arizona to start our own business, choosing spiritual beliefs and spirituality as a high value. Choosing loyalty, honesty, and integrity within the family unit, and choosing to have a high respect for each other as individuals. I told her what each of our children was doing and how we valued higher education. I told her about our family life, what we liked to eat, and what we did on our vacations.

When I finished, I nervously checked my watch and realized there were now at least twenty-five people crowded around listening.

"Could I have that picture? I would keep it forever," she told me as I started to say good-bye. Her sweet smile and wet eyes stayed in my mind, as we hugged and left.

Can you imagine? A lady in China has our family's picture, because it represents unlimited choices which she could never even dream of making with her own family. Perhaps it also represents hope for her future! The whole time I talked to her I realized how few choices she had and how fortunate we are to have so many. Every choice we make has incredible, long-range consequences, and I believe it is important to make the right choice and then to keep making your choice right. It is an ongoing process.

Each family unit is faced with innumerable choices: We can choose to share our lives with each other, to respect each other, to commit to each other, to work together for a common goal, to love each other, and to forgive each other. Or we can choose the opposite and make our family life miserable, or even nonexistent.

Freedom of choice . . . one of our most precious and least appreciated gifts.

THE CHRISTIAN HOME is the Master's workshop where the processes of character molding are silently, lovingly, faithfully, and successfully carried on.

RICHARD MONCKTON MILNES

THE FAMILY WAS ordained of God that children might be trained up for himself; it was before the church, or rather the first form of the church on earth. POPE LEO XIII

GIVE YOUR CHILDREN up to God. . . . it is utterly safe to place your children in God's sure hands. JOHN WHITE

CIVILIZATION VARIES WITH the family, and the family with civilization. Its highest and most complete realization is found where enlightened Christianity prevails; where woman is exalted to her true and lofty place as equal with the man; where husband and wife are one in honor, influence, and affection, and where children are a common bond of care and love. This is the idea of a perfect family.

WILLIAM AIKMAN

TOO MANY OF today's children have straight teeth and crooked morals. A HIGH SCHOOL PRINCIPAL

MANY PARENTS DO nothing about their children's religious education, telling them they can decide what they believe when they're twenty-one. That's like telling them they can decide when they're twenty-one whether or not they should brush their teeth. By then, their teeth may have fallen out. Likewise, their principles and morality may also be non-existent. PRINCESS GRACE OF MONACO

# • *Shaping Children's Behavior* •

Home is where life makes up its mind.
HAZEN WERNER

*E*rynn Ruth loved to amuse her parents by carrying out their instructions to the letter. When her dad said, "You stay right there and don't move," Erynn would assume a motionless stance and not even blink an eyelid. If her mom said, "Go pick up your room," Erynn would reply, "But Mom, it's too heavy. I can't pick up my room." Being a literalist is fine sometimes, but one day Erynn came across a situation she literally didn't know how to handle.

At a friend's birthday party Erynn was served a hot dog and root beer. Not sure what to do, she asked the hostess if she could use the phone.

"Mom," Erynn asked, "am I allowed to drink root beer?"

Obviously, in Erynn's mind root beer must have some connection with beer, which she knew her family didn't drink. Although she had never been offered root beer before, she assumed she'd better not drink any without asking.

This was only a small incident in a child's life, but it offers major insight into the importance of a parent's values and standards and how they influence children.

A similar situation happened to Somer. Her mother had never given her any food laden with processed sugar. However, in gymnastics class Somer was awarded a candy bar for her good performance. Somer wasn't sure whether to be happy or sad.

"What's a candy bar?" Somer asked her stunned gymnastics teacher.

As parents we sometimes forget the tremendous responsibility we have in shaping our children's lives. Little children's minds are like sponges, soaking up everything they see and hear. Until they reach the age of reason, they take at face value everything they are told by someone they trust or admire. Children are carefully watching and absorbing our every action and reaction, our standards and beliefs or lack of them, and applying our rules of conduct to their own lives.

I was touched when my niece Kary told me she had been tucking her own niece into bed for years, just as I had done with her, and saying, "This is the way my Aunt Naomi used to tuck me in." No special techniques, just lots of love and a little back tickling—and our every action teaches our loved ones behavior patterns which they in turn pass on to their loved ones.

It is the sum total of a child's experiences that determine his destiny, including his heredity as well as his home life, his friends, his education, his church, his recreation, his job, his wife or husband, plus the books and magazines he reads, the films he sees, the television he watches. Our children are a composite of all these, some of which are beyond our control.

ROBERT HASTINGS

# • *Is a Child Ever Too Young to Learn?* •

BY THE TIME children are five, their parents will have done at least half of all that can ever be done to determine the children's future faith.                    RANDOLPH MILLER

THINKING THAT THREE hours of any movie are harmless for the child but two hours of church and Sunday School are too much for his nervous system is just bad thinking. Giving him a nickel for the collection and a dollar for the movies not only shows a parent's sense of value but is also likely to produce a proportionate giver.            *ZION'S HERALD*

# • *The Price of Commitment* •

*W*hat is your family committed to? Are you committed to building your dream home? Retiring at an early age? Reaching a certain income level or social status? Committed to achieving a certain position of power or prominence? Are you committed to each other? To the protection and fulfillment of each family member? To supporting each other and helping each other? Are you committed to giving your children the best possible home life? Are you committed to their education? Are you committed to your religious beliefs and values? Are you committed to your marriage? To parenting? Or is your primary commitment to your career, money, power, or status?

When you commit to your family, you stick with them regardless of unforeseen circumstances, physical or mental problems, substance abuse, negative attitudes, reckless spending habits, personality problems, insecurities, or outside interference. It includes sustaining the loss of a family member, your job, youth, health, or anything else you deeply care about.

Commitment is necessary in life to see a project through to completion. Your family is a project given to you by God. Your commitment to your family is going to determine the happiness and outcome of your family. Commitment is part of the support system that holds your family together. It's always going to cost more than you anticipated. Are you willing to pay the price?

Times get rough when you are raising a family or are just part of a family. Things don't always turn out the way you anticipated. Strong families learn to adapt. They change their priorities. They reassess their values. They put the needs of their family above their own individual desires. They find ways to communicate when communication seems impossible.

Commitment is required to build families. It involves being willing to pay the price in terms of time, money, and lives.

Hopefully, you won't need to literally give your life for your family, but you do need to give your family your time, your energies, your personality, your gifts, your talents, and most of all, your love. Without commitment to your family, your dreams for them will never become a reality.

IN AN EFFORT to ensure my children's tomorrows, I have lost their todays. DANNY THOMAS

DON'T TELL ME how much you love me; show me by having time for me. ULRICH SCHAFFER

THE GREAT MAN is he who dares not lose his child's heart. MENCIUS

I HAVEN'T COMPLETELY figured out being a parent by any means. The one thing I do know is that the bottom line is love—they have to know you love them. ROGER STAUBACH

MONEY, STATUS, CAREER, power, and a thousand other pursuits may burn brightly for a time in our lives. But when winds of reflection clear away the smoke, nothing satisfies or fulfills a man more profoundly than the genuine love and praise of his children. PAUL LEWIS

A FAMOUS MAN is one whose children love him. UNKNOWN

## • *Our Happy Home* •

*T*here are many different kinds of homes,
But I thank God for one;
The happy place where I can go
When my day is done.
Some homes are built on sinking sand
Without a good foundation
But Jesus is our cornerstone,
He has an open invitation,
To visit us at any time
From morning til close of day;
I thank God for our happy home,
For He's made it that way.

DARLENE BLACKMON

# • *Homemade Children* •

*A*s I write this recipe there is bread "raising" on my hearth—and children "raising" in my home. The end product is not yet finished, but the ingredients have been carefully selected, measured, and blended. The "Recipe Book" promises: "Train up a child in the way he should go, And when he is old, he will not depart from it" (Proverbs 22:6). Having followed other recipes in this book, I trust the Author!

MEASURE into a home two parents who love each other and a few children (use own discretion on number; we prefer three).

ADD yeast, stirring constantly (we recommend only one brand, Jesus Christ).

STIR in:

wisdom—as much as possible from God's Word, previous training, and lots of common sense
truth—very important for consistent results
patience—ample portions needed throughout
kindness—large volumes
gentleness—soften before adding
discipline—with fairness, measured in a clean container
love—full measure, pressed down, shaken together, and overflowing the cup
laughter—knead in as much as possible, and let it permeate throughout the whole batch

All ingredients should be measured using a container of prayer—make no substitutes for prayer.

For excellent taste and preserving quality, keep dough as soft and pliable as possible, but not too sticky, so you, with God's help, can handle it.

Mix till smooth and elastic (about eighteen years), round up in a greased bowl (with life's struggles), and cover with a damp cloth (with failures as well as victories).

Let rise in a *warm* place (the environmental temperature is very important) until double in size (about four to eight years after high school).

Dough will be ready to be divided and made into all shapes of beautiful men and women to be used as "bread" (the Staff of Life) for other people's lives.

Guaranteed—godly results!

## • *The Love Chapter through a Parent's Eyes* •

*If* I have the gift of speaking Spanish and French fluently, and the gift of communicating to friends, business associates, and Sunday School classes, but don't take time to say "I love you; Have a beautiful day; You're special" to my children, I am a clanging gong, a worthless whistle.

If I have the gift of being a great planner of the future, a cum laude graduate, a positive thinker with abundant faith in God, but lack the daily encouragement and interest in my children's current goals and hurts, I am missing my highest calling.

If I am a faithful tither, giving extra gifts for specific needs, and if I am willing to donate my body parts upon death, but I can't give my children access to my resources in providing a Christ-centered education and can't give to them my legs and arms to play with them, my ears (and mouth) to share love secrets, and my heart to share life with—then all this is hollow and meaningless.

Love is patience while you wait in the parking lot after school; love is kind to all sorts of friends; love is not jealous of awards they win in life that we didn't; love does not puff up the truth or take the full credit for neat kids.

Loving parents do not always put their interests and time above their children's. They don't transgress rudely their children's privacy and their need to have secrets to share when they want to. They do not embarrass their children in front of friends and don't keep an everlasting scorebook to remind their children of past failures.

Loving parents are happy to find that their children were right and they were wrong in a discussion when this is indeed the truth.

Love means exhibiting the power of expectation with our children. We will believe in them, support them, defend them, and recognize that the portrait of their lives isn't finished being painted yet, especially on days when there is a low grade, a crabby spirit, a broken friendship, or a lost contact lens. Love gives, gives, and gives once more and is an irresistible force in our children's motivation.

Faith, Hope, Love, these three; but the greatest of these is Love.

# • *A Stepping Stone or a Stumbling Block?* •

*I*sn't it strange that princes and
   kings
And clowns that caper in sawdust
   rings
And common folk like you and me
Are builders for eternity?

To each is given a book of rules
A block of stone and a bag of tools
For each must shape ere time has
   flown
A stumbling block or a stepping
   stone.

UNKNOWN


When I approach a child, he inspires in me two sentiments:
tenderness for what he is, and respect for what he may become.                                                LOUIS PASTEUR

TRAIN UP A child in a way he should go—and walk there yourself once in a while.

JOSH BILLINGS

CHILDREN SELDOM MISQUOTE you. They more often repeat word for word what you shouldn't have said.

MAE MALOO

IF YOU WANT your boy to follow in your footsteps, you've probably forgotten a few you took.

UNKNOWN

MY GREATEST ANNOUNCEMENT to the world is really my kids. I think that makes or breaks what I talk about.

CHUCK SWINDOLL

SOMEDAY, SOMEWHERE, I shall see what my life has come to mean to those who have watched me live.

VIRGIL REED (MY FATHER)

A FATHER SHOULD be a blessing to his children in more than sharing thoughts and intellectual communication. The father passes on a blessing to his wife and children by the way he walks.

LUIS PALAU

WHEN THEY'VE SEEN me do something wrong, I must quickly go to them to apologize and seek forgiveness. It's what they must see me model if they are going to mature into sensitive persons, able to admit and set right their mistakes.

JOSH MCDOWELL

# • *Being a Model for Our Children* •

Children learn first and best from their families. Just as by
the end of the second year their language is that of the
people with whom they live, so their behavior is
stamped with the seal of their adult protectors.

SADIE GINSBERG

*E*verything we do or don't do is a model for our children.
We can't fool kids. They are aware of our attitudes at levels
that we don't even observe sometimes ourselves. Children
mimic their parents and decide what they want or don't want
to be based upon what they see in us.

Subconsciously they pick up our habits and actions and
pass them down from generation to generation. The old story
about the young bride cutting off the ends of her ham before
she put it in the baking dish always amuses me. When her
husband asked her why she did it, she said, "Because I always
saw my mother do it." When his mother in-law came over for
dinner, he asked her why she always cut the ends off her ham
before she baked it. "Because my mother always did it," she
replied. Finally Grandma came over for dinner and the young
groom asked her why she always cut the ends off her ham
before she baked it. Giving him a weird look she said, "Because I only had one baking dish and the ham wouldn't fit in
it."

Logic doesn't always play a part in our actions. If our parents did it, we frequently assume it's what we're supposed to
do. Accepting without questioning is the basis of most model-
ing, and it starts at a very early age.

Realizing how much our children absorb from our actions
and attitudes, we must not only serve as good models for our
children but also surround them with friends, peers, and associates who provide good models also. What kinds of guests do
we invite into our homes to share their lives with our observ-
ant children? Do we expose them to a wide variety of people
with various levels of professional, career, financial, spiritual,
intellectual, social, political, and personal commitments?

Or do we try to teach them that our way is the only way?

> Children have more need of models than of critics.
>
> JOSEPH JOUBERT

## • *Teaching by Example* •

*E*ducation does not mean teaching people what they do not know. It means teaching them to behave as they do not behave. It is not teaching the youth the shapes of letters and the tricks of numbers, and then leaving them to turn their arithmetic to roguery, and their literature to lust. It means, on the contrary, training them into the perfect exercise and kingly continence of their bodies and souls. It is a painful, continual, and difficult work to be done by kindness, by watching, by warning, by precept, and by praise, but above all—by example. JOHN RUSKIN

# • *A Religious Foundation* •

A sense of Deity is inscribed on every heart.
JOHN CALVIN

*S*trong and healthy families have in common a shared core of religious beliefs. Spiritual beliefs or lack of them will influence every area of your family life—the way you reach out to and treat others, the way you handle conflict and anger, and the way you practice forgiveness. It provides the support and strength and meaning for all activities, purposes, and goals.

Your religious beliefs will contribute to your family's sense of identity, create a sense of belonging, and assist in character development. I believe a healthy self-concept is only possible in a person who genuinely feels loved and accepted as a child of God. Knowing we are loved by someone so wonderful as God makes it easier to believe we are worthy of love. We have a reason for our existence, something to make all our labors worthwhile, as well as peace about life after death.

Our family's spiritual beliefs are a part of our daily interaction, as well as our social life. Prayer before meals and about family problems and concerns, weekly church services, and a nurturing support system of fellow believers for our children—people who believed as we do to help nurture our children—these provided a healthy atmosphere for our family. I believe inscribing the sense of Deity described by Calvin to be the God-given responsibility of parents.

## • *I'd Rather See a Sermon* •
. . . . . . . . . . . . . . . . . . . . . . . . . . . . .

*I'*d rather see a sermon than hear one any day
I'd rather one should walk with me than merely show the
   way.
The eye's a better pupil and more willing than the ear;
Fine counsel is confusing, but example's always clear;
And the best of all the preachers are the men who live their
   creeds,
For to see the good in action is what everybody needs.
I can soon learn how to do it if you'll let me see it done.
I can watch your hands in action, but your tongue too fast
   may run;
And the lectures you deliver may be very wise and true,
But I'd rather get my lesson by observing what you do.
For I may misunderstand you and the high advice you
   give,
But there's no misunderstanding how you act and how you
   live.

UNKNOWN

# • *The Gift of Honor* •

Be kindly affectionate to one another with brotherly
love, in honor giving preference to one another.
ROMANS 12:10

*F*rom the very beginning of his dating relationship with
Beth, our son-in-law Curt honored our daughter and our en-
tire family. He always found a way to make us feel like an
important part of their lives, including asking our permission
to marry Beth. Little did we know that Curt intended to make
us such an important part of his proposal.

During our traditional back-to-school party for all school-
going members of our family, Curt pulled Jim aside and told
him, "I have the ring, Dad, and I would like for you to be the
one to give it to Beth." What an incredible gift of honor!

At the end of our meal and after everyone received their
back-to-school gift, Curt said, "I have one more gift" and he
pulled a seashell out of his pocket for Beth. All Curt's family
are deep-sea divers and collect rare shells. Throughout their
courtship Curt had given Beth shells with special notes tucked
inside. Beth pulled a note out of this shell which read, "Will
you marry me?"

Beth started to cry and passed the little note and shell
around the family circle so everyone could read it. Everyone
had tears in their eyes at this special moment, and Jim handed
Beth a napkin to wipe her eyes, saying, "You'd better look
inside the napkin." Much to her surprise, she found her engagement ring tucked inside.

Curt's gift of honor to Jim recognized the special bond of
love between Jim and Beth. By presenting the diamond to
Beth, Jim symbolized his approval of the marriage.

*T*he family is a little book,
   The children are the leaves,
The parents are the cover that
   Safe protection gives.

At first, the pages of the book
   Are blank, and smooth, and fair;
But time soon writeth memories,
   And painteth pictures there.

Love is the golden clasp
   That bindeth up the trust;
O break it not, lest all the leaves
   Shall scatter like the dust.

UNKNOWN

·················

# PART THREE

# *Family Essentials*

·················

# • *The Strength of a Family* •
. . . . . . . . . . . . . . . . . . . . . . . . . . .

Dialogue takes place when people communicate the full
meaning of their lives to one another, when they
participate in each other's lives in the most
meaningful ways in which they are capable.

DWIGHT SMALL

*F*amilies are easier to create than maintain. Someone must
accept the responsibility for the family's welfare, be disciplined enough to pay the price, and willing to devote the necessary time to do the work.

Responsibility is a key factor in maintaining families for
both parents and children. Responsible children are a product
of responsible adults. Disciplined parents raise disciplined
children. And it is not a once-a-year or once-a-month event; it
is a daily activity.

Fortunately, just spending time with your family doing the
ordinary chores of living and enjoying being together is most
important. Time together strengthens family ties. Planned
times together and unplanned times together, quality time together and not-so-high quality time together—it all adds up to
keeping the family strong.

And what's essential? Traditions. Respect. Celebrations.
Laughter. Togetherness. Responsibility. Forgiveness. Discipline. Acceptance. Our family was built out of materials and
concepts that might not suit your family's life-style or values.
However, I believe you can take some of our materials and
ideas and adapt them to your own use. What's essential for
your family is something only you can decide.

What greater thing is there for human souls than to feel
that they are joined for life—to strengthen each other in all
labor, to rest on each other in all sorrow, to minister to each
other in all pain, and to be with each other in silent unspeak-
able memories . . .                          GEORGE ELIOT

# • *Our House* •

The walls of our house are not built of wood, brick, or stone, but of truth and loyalty.

Unpleasant sounds of grumbling, the friction of living, the clash of personalities, are not deadened by Persian rugs or polished floors, but by conciliation, and concession. . . .

Our house is not a structure where bodies meet, but a hearthstone upon which flames mingle, separate flames of souls, which, the more perfectly they unite, the more clearly they shine and the straighter they rise toward heaven.

Our house is a fortress in a warring world, where loving hands buckle on your armor in the morning and soothe your fatigue and wounds at night.

> The beauty of our house is harmony.
> The security of our house is loyalty.
> The joy of our house is love.
> The plenty of our house is in children.
> The rule of our house is service.
> The comfort of our house is in contented spirits.
> The maker of our house, a real human house, is
>     God Himself, the same who made the stars
>     and built the world.

UNKNOWN

# • *Our Family* •
. . . . . . . . . . . . . . . . .

*O*ur family is a blessing;
It means so many things.
Words could never really tell
The joy our family brings.
Our family is mutual love,
The love of Dad and Mother
Showing children how to love
And care for one another.
Our family is heartfelt pride,
The feeling deep and strong
That makes us glad to take a part
And know that we belong.
Our family is always home,
A place where we can share
Our joys and sorrow, hopes and dreams
For happiness lives there.
Our family is a bond of faith
That even time can't sever.
A gift to last throughout our lives,
The family of God is forever.

UNKNOWN

# • Establishing Family Traditions •

Traditions and rituals give importance to a moment, a
sense of grace. They allow us to acknowledge an
important moment or change in our lives.

JAY O'CALLAHAN

*W*hen my mother married, her Icelandic mother, my
*Amma*, took some wool from the sheep on their farm, carded
and spun it, and then made a quilt as a wedding gift for my
parents. My mom and dad used it until Dad died; then
Mother chose not to sleep under it without him. When I got
married, she re-covered the quilt and passed it on to me. After
twenty-four years, the quilt pulled apart and needed to be re-
done. I divided the wool inside into three parts, and when
each one of our children was married I had a quilt made with
the original wool in it. Each of our kids had a part of that quilt
under which my mom and dad slept all of their married life
and under which my husband and I slept most of our married
life. When Mother gave the quilt to Jim and me, she said it
was more than a quilt—it was a "comforter." It was a reminder of my parents' love, warmth, and care, since they
couldn't always be with us. This "gift of continuity and care"
was one we wanted to pass on to our children in their new
homes.

If you're humming "Tradition" and pretending to be
Tevye in *Fiddler on the Roof,* you're on the right track. Tradition is that sense of continuity, wholeness, immovability,
changelessness, and stability, that single thread which unites
and which brings comfort in lives bombarded by unceasing,
unpredictable change. The world is moving fast, and we need
a sense of belonging, a center, a history, and a future we can
depend on. Actively maintaining tradition by giving it to your
family provides such a center.

Traditions don't need to be expensive, but they are one of
the greatest gifts you can give to your family. Our family traditions included family hugs, when all five of us would come
together and hold hands and pray and hug one another. Physi-

cal expression of love is a valuable tradition to pass on to your children, who hopefully will practice it with their families.

The children made a tradition of climbing in bed with us every Saturday morning when they woke up. Although it eventually became rather crowded, it was a fun and warm way to start our weekend times of relaxation together. Now, our five grandsons carry on this tradition when they visit us.

Each Tuesday night was family night. And each week a different family member planned the dinner menu. After dinner we had a family meeting and discussed the family calendar, any problems or concerns, and played games, sang, and laughed together. "Rhode Games" were our favorite! Any member of the family could think of a question that the other members would then answer. Two of my favorites were: If you could spend one day with any person who has ever lived, who would it be and why? And, if you could be a drop of water in any form, anywhere in the world, what would it be and where?

One very important tradition in our family life was based upon our religious convictions: We said a blessing before every meal, often had family devotions together, and attended church every Sunday morning and Sunday night. We wanted to model that spiritual belief is a lifestyle, not a one-day-a-week ritual; it's a tradition we wanted to pass on to our children as part of their rich heritage.

Twice a year on Memorial Day and Labor Day we had family planning sessions. We ate a big breakfast on the patio and planned our individual and family activities for the summer or the next year. We chose a verse from Scripture and memorized it as our family theme for the next few months. Each of us created a ten-year plan for our lives. We evaluated our progress each year and made adjustments for the coming year. Looking back over our lives and seeing how many of our goals were reached, we realize how significant those planning sessions were in our lives and what a meaningful tradition it was for us, one we hope our children will carry on with their families.

Traditions can be as insignificant as having hamburgers every Saturday night or the popcorn party Jim threw once a year for all the kids' friends. I know one mother whose children ate a balanced meal three times a day, six days a week. However, on Saturdays she let them eat anything they wanted—whether it was a bowl of cake icing, raw cookie dough for breakfast, or six kinds of junk food. Of course, they also had to live with the consequences, but the kids, now grown, look back and laugh at their tradition.

Webster defines *tradition* as "the handing down of information, beliefs, and customs by word of mouth or by example from one generation to another without written instruction." It's not terrifically important what the tradition is, other than your values and beliefs, just that your family has some.

Long after Jim and I are gone, I believe the traditions we established and practiced in our family life will live on and serve as a warm memory of our love and affection.

# • *Some Traditions Aren't All That Great* •

> Our acts make or mar us—we are the
> children of our own deeds.
> VICTOR HUGO

*D*uring my childhood days we had a little white dog with a black spot. Regardless of what Rascal did and even when he grew old and feeble, I loved him dearly.

When I was in the sixth grade, my father had emergency surgery. When my mother told me that my dad almost died, she also told me she had put Rascal to sleep.

It was one of the saddest days of my life. Not only did I feel insecure about the possibility of losing my father, but I felt betrayed that my mother hadn't asked me about putting Rascal to sleep or allowed me to see him before he died.

In later years I didn't want my children to have a dog, perhaps because of the deep sense of loss I felt over Rascal. I didn't even want an animal around the house. However, for my thirty-third birthday my nephew Kevin gave me a dog which we named Adam. The kids were crazy about Adam, and I immediately fell in love with him too. Adam was our constant companion for eleven years.

Then we moved to a new home that didn't have a fenced yard and wasn't going to have one. By this time we were traveling frequently, Mark and Beth no longer lived at home, and Katherine would graduate from high school in one year. Without Katherine's agreement, I gave Adam away to our former next-door neighbor who had loved and cared for Adam.

History had repeated itself. Call it a tradition or call it insensitivity, but I deeply hurt Katherine's feelings just as my mother had hurt mine. Without even thinking about it, often we not only carry on good traditions but also some sad ones.

Just as a healthy legacy is passed down, so is an unhealthy legacy. Since Adam and Eve, parents have found it easier to pass on their sins to their children than to pass on their virtues. The weaknesses and shortcomings of the parents are often repeated in the children. If the parents are negative, self-destructive, and hostile, their children carry with them into adulthood a bitter harvest of inner conflicts.

Although my family tree passed down a wonderful spiritual heritage to their descendants, the sins were also passed down. One of my greatest heartbreaks in life is my unsuccessful attempt to overcome the heritage of isolation and the glass wall of indifference that has been built up between some members of my family for four generations. I continually pray that this tragedy can be stopped in my generation and if not, that my children will be able to prevent this great sorrow in their generation.

## • *Family Ties* •

*F*amily ties are precious things
   Woven through the years
Of memories of togetherness . . .
   Of laughter, love and tears.

Family ties are cherished things
   Forged in childhood days
By love of parents, deep and true,
   And sweet familiar ways.

Family ties are treasured things,
   And far though we may roam,
The tender bonds with those we love
   Still pull our hearts toward home.

VIRGINIA BLANCK MOORE

# • *Celebrate Life* •

Confront the diversity of your generation, learn to live
with that diversity, and ultimately come to celebrate it.
DONALD KENNEDY

*I*f anything describes the Rhode family, it is celebrations.
We look for excuses to have them. The occasion might be as
minor as a good grade or as significant as a wedding, but we
do try to celebrate as many aspects of our lives as possible.
Celebrate the ordinary parts of life, not just the extraordinary.
The reality is that the ordinary is all around us and in the
ordinary we can find tremendous cause for wonderful celebration and memories. You can choose to celebrate your family
life by these means:

- capitalizing on your areas of unity,
- appreciating your areas of uniqueness,
- enjoying life and all it has to offer,
- finding things to laugh about together,
- working on a mutual purpose for your lives,
- encouraging emotional health in each other,
- building each other's self-esteem,
- developing better communication skills,
- basking in the healing qualities of comraderie,
- maximizing strengths and minimizing weaknesses,
- expressing anger in the right way,
- resolving conflicts in a healthy manner,
- avoiding actions which lead to loss of trust, and
- freely forgiving others as you want to be forgiven.

Although I don't know the details of your family life, I do
know that we can all celebrate life and the beauty of every
precious moment. Celebrations should be a part of everyday
life and certainly of successful, healthy families. Enjoy celebrating. Look for things to celebrate!

# • *Celebrate Your Love* •

For over thirty years Jim and I have celebrated June 15, 1957. We were married on a nice warm Minnesota day in an ivy-covered chapel by a wonderful, caring pastor, Erwin Butler, with family and dear friends witnessing the event. Our first dinner as a married couple was at the Anoka Steak House. It may sound very ordinary to you, but it was very special to us.

Jim and I have celebrated literally thousands of times in our marriage and family life; some were elaborate and many were mini-celebrations. But none heralds my joy more than remembering the celebration of the beginning of our love and marriage and those of our children, to celebrate what we trust will be long, happy married lives.

The wedding of our daughter Beth and her husband, Curt, was our first glimpse of what it is like to link another family eternally to ours. Because both families had spent a lot of time in Hawaii while the kids were growing up, Beth and Curt chose to use Hawaiian flowers and celebrate their marriage with a festival of classical and spiritual music. As a part of the marriage ceremony, the pastor read love letters Beth and Curt had written to their parents, a celebration of "giving back" to us in a very dear way. What an emotional surprise!

Mark and Melody's wedding was marked by serendipity: Mark chose one of our adult friends to be an attendant, Melody asked her sister from Paris to sing, a small black choir offered two marvelous spirituals, the reception took place in a beautiful garden, and a horse-and-buggy carried the bride and groom from the church. Probably my favorite part of their celebration was the worship service the night before the wedding day for the wedding party and the out-of-town guests. They desired to shift the emphasis for that evening away from themselves and to God who had so abundantly blessed them at this special time of unity. I will never forget hearing strangers stand and share that they had prayed for the person that Melody would marry since she was a little girl. What a heritage to know that person was our son, Mark!

When Katherine married Ken, their celebration theme was Numbers 10:10: "In the day of your gladness . . . blow the trumpets." Trumpeters preceded them down the aisle. Brass trumpets decorated the rehearsal party and the reception, and the church bulletins had trumpets on them. We had coffee mugs made with the logo and theme, Ken and Katherine's name, and marriage date. Each person who came to the celebration the evening before received one and was asked to pray for Ken and Katherine when they used the mug. Since their wedding I often meet people who say, "I use that mug every morning for my breakfast coffee, and I pray for Ken and Katherine." What shared power to bring your extended family and friends into the celebration!

As you build into your children the concept of celebrating joy and teach them to plan for others' enjoyment as well, a priceless gift comes to you.

Two weeks before our twenty-fifth wedding anniversary our children surprised us with a celebration that took four typewritten pages of instruction and twenty college kids to accomplish. A chauffeured limousine ushered us to a series of friends' homes for a progressive dinner, with surprise couples in each home who had flown in from around the country for the celebration.

After dessert in a friend's gazebo, we were escorted to a room to find my wedding gown hung clean and pressed and a tuxedo for Jim. Buttoning twenty-five little satin buttons around a few extra pounds caused some consternation. We were driven to a helicopter landing pad at the airport. There stood our best man and matron of honor, Don and Jan from Minnesota, with a scrapbook of our marriage, a party invitation, and helping hands into the helicopter.

On our wedding day Jim had wanted to surprise me by renting a helicopter but I had refused because I had never flown in one and was afraid. However, when the children rented one for us twenty-five years later, I was willing. The helicopter took us across the city and started circling over our neighborhood. We looked down in amazement to see lines of cars, droves of people, and a beautiful red carpet from our house to the street.

Two hundred fifty people greeted our arrival. There were speeches and music, wonderful wedding cake and gifts, surprise telephone calls, and reminiscing over fond memories.

A special resort was our destination for the weekend. The children had packed our suitcase and included fourteen cassettes from various couples around the country, telling us how much they valued our lives and relationship.

The celebration we started in an ivy-covered chapel returned to us from children who had learned to value, anticipate, and love the whole concept of celebrating. We celebrate not only the ordinary but the extraordinary with a deep sense of abiding love.

# • *Celebrate in Everything* •

For the wise man, every day is a festival.
PLUTARCH

*E*aster is a significant holiday for the Rhode family, and we do everything possible to be together as a family then. Several years ago, we planned a spectacular celebration—twenty-one family members and dear friends joined us for brunch under our new gazebo. Our children and their spouses were coming from all over the United States to be with us for the occasion.

Katherine and Ken arrived from Minnesota on Thursday. Beth and our grandson Dathan were to arrive on Good Friday. Beth's husband, Curt, would join us on Sunday. The anticipation of a wonderful family celebration filled the air.

Then the call came, as Beth and Dathan were supposed to be boarding their plane. Dathan was ill and with deep regret and remorse, they would have to miss our much-awaited Easter celebration and family reunion.

Beth was in tears. She would miss seeing her sister, everyone was going to be having fun without her, and she would be home alone on Easter with a sick child and a husband working at the hospital all weekend. I felt deep frustration as I hung up the phone.

Then Katherine and I looked at each other and we knew what we had to do. She made reservations for a quick trip to Los Angeles with inexpensive fun fare tickets. I grabbed a picnic basket, threw in everything I could find for lunch, grabbed some flowers and a great music box for Dathan. We'd stay two and a half hours, and make it home for our obligations that evening. We raced to the airport, jumped on the plane, and we were off.

A depressed and dreary Beth answered the door at our knock. Her shock soon turned to excitement when she realized she wasn't dreaming. For two incredible hours we had a wonderful reunion and exchanged the gifts of love and encouragement which she so desperately needed and we will never forget.

But that's not the end of the story. After a great Friday, I worked all day Saturday getting the food and tables ready for Sunday. I decorated the new gazebo like a scene out of *House Beautiful*.

Then I hurt my back, and all Saturday night I suffered, wondering if I could go through with the brunch on Sunday. Easter Sunday morning arrived with the worst rainstorm Arizona had experienced in several months.

I was miserable, really feeling sorry for myself. I was in pain, couldn't walk, and now it was raining. Should I just cancel the celebration and go to bed with an ice pack? Or should I choose to have a different attitude about the weather, my new gazebo, my ruined party plans, and my sore back?

Fortunately, I remembered Friday and Beth. And I changed my plans and moved the celebration inside, regardless of my pain.

And what a wonderful celebration it turned out to be! All during lunch the torrential downpour continued, but we were enjoying the warmth and security of our friendship and love inside the house. As the last guests said goodbye, the now empty clouds dumped their last few sprinkles on us and gently floated away, leaving in their place a gorgeous rainbow.

What a fool I would have been to cancel the brunch because my plans had been "ruined" by my back and the rain. Life doesn't always turn out according to our plans and expectations, but we make minor adjustments and go on without feeling sorry for ourselves. Otherwise we miss out on so much that we are meant to enjoy.

It's the same with our family life. We enter with high expectations, but something happens that upsets our plans or cuts us off emotionally from the festivities. Sound familiar? Of course, it happens to all of us; every family has imperfect people, complicated relationships, and unfortunate circumstances.

Celebrations don't always turn out the way we anticipated, but we make alternative plans which can result in even greater happiness. Life is a celebration, and families need to celebrate. Look for the rainbow in the storm clouds as a promise of a new beginning. Remember it takes both sunshine and rain to make a rainbow.

After the darkness the daylight shines through
After the showers the rainbow's in view
After life's heartaches there comes from above
The peace and the comfort of God's healing love

UNKNOWN

# • *Respecting Need for Privacy* •

*W*hen Beth was in the fifth grade, she begged to have a room of her own. Our house wasn't big enough for her to have a real room, but Jim did have an office area about the size of a large closet which he gave up so Beth could have more privacy. Her twin bed totally filled three of the walls but there was a tiny area left over which we made into a closet.

Beth selected matching wallpaper and fabric for her bedspread and canopy. Although it was small, her cherished room afforded her the privacy she needed and assured her of our respect for her needs.

Jim brought home a poster with a ship on it and the saying, "A ship in harbor is safe but that isn't what ships are built for." Every morning he would wake Beth up with the words from the poster, rub her back, tell her what a great day she was going to have, and encourage her to go out and pursue life to its fullest.

Even if you don't have a separate area for each child, each child needs a place to call his or her own. Maybe it's just a chest of drawers or a single drawer or a box that no one else is allowed to examine, a place for their cherished dreams and possessions. Privacy affirms a child's identity and the right to personal dignity—a right parents should not violate.

> In their eagerness for their children to acquire skills and to succeed, parents may forget that youngsters need time to think, and privacy in which to do it.          JAMES COX

# • *Communication* •
. . . . . . . . . . . . . . . . . . .

There's no way I can keep my body in shape unless I practice at least three, four, or five times a week. Family relationships are exactly the same. You can't store them. Like exercise, they're an ongoing type of thing.

In aerobic conditioning, we say it's got to be at least thirty minutes, three times a week. And it can't be just a blasé thirty minutes; it's got to be a good thirty minutes. You must get the heart rate up. The same is true in the family. Thirty minutes, three times a week, in strictly 100 percent family communication and family relationship, and you experience a wonderful growth in the family's strength and health.

KENNETH H. COOPER, M.D.

...........................................

Family jokes, though rightly cursed by strangers,
are the bond that keeps most families alive.
STELLA BENSON

*O*ur family never tolerated profanity. Jim and I set the example, and the children didn't deviate from the rule.

Except once.

On one of our family trips it seemed like an eternity before we arrived at our destination, Hoover Dam. The temperature was well into the 100s and nothing we did could cool the car. One unfortunate incident after another seemed to delay our arrival. Finally, after six hours in the car, we pulled into the visitor's parking lot.

"Boy, am I ever glad to be in this Dam parking lot," Jim sighed.

Total silence prevailed; we looked at one another with our mouths open.

Then hysteria set in. The kids thought they had caught their dad swearing. Everyone laughed and laughed and laughed and laughed.

"But I meant the *Hoover Dam* parking lot," Jim vainly tried to explain. "It's okay to say 'Dam' if you are talking about a particular Dam like Hoover Dam."

Inadvertently, Jim had given them permission to say "Dam" that day. Never have any visitors laughed so much as our family did as we toured the Dam.

"Boy, this *Dam* elevator sure is nice," Mark reported. We all laughed.

"Yes, and this *Dam* color is very unusual," chimed in Beth. We laughed some more.

"I wonder how many cars this *Dam* parking lot holds?" Katherine asked. More gales of laughter followed.

During the whole tour the kids found an incredible number of things to comment on with the word *Dam* . . . meaning Hoover, of course.

Silly? Yes. Funny? Yes. Maybe not to you, but to our family it was hysterical because their father had "violated" one of our household's sacred rules and they could follow his example and take advantage of his apparent slipup.

It's a private joke, but one which never fails to bring laughter to all of us, even fifteen years later, anytime we think about it or mention it. Families need private jokes. Things to laugh about that no one else understands or appreciates. Private jokes and shared laughter is one of the bonds that holds a family together.

## • *A Laugh a Day* •

A WELL-DEVELOPED SENSE of humor is the pole that adds balance to your steps as you walk the tightrope of life.

WILLIAM A. WARD

A MAN WITH a sense of humor doesn't make jokes out of life; he merely recognizes the ones that are there.

*NUGGETS*

THE ABILITY TO get a laugh out of everyday situations is a safety valve, ridding you of tensions which might otherwise damage your health. *WEEKEND*

WITH THE FEARFUL strain that is on me night and day, if I did not laugh I should die. ABRAHAM LINCOLN

TWO QUALITIES—LAUGHTER and love—are vital to bridging the generation gap. . . . Too many of the young have forgotten how to laugh . . . and too many of their elders have forgotten how to love. *EDUCATION SUMMARY*

# • *Spending Time Together* •

Parents have given kids so much in order to buy their love
and respect that they've blown everything. What's
really bad is that they don't even realize there
is a generation gap. The bridge can only
be built with love that isn't bought.

MIKE COPE, TEENAGER

"*L*ove that isn't bought." What an incredible phrase!
What insight! Frequently parents do try to buy children's love
and respect by giving them more material possessions and
benefits than they want or need. What children really need is
time with their parents.

When our children were small, Jim's job required a lot of
travel; so we bought a station wagon and traveled together.
Each child had a favorite seat/bed. Katherine always took the
back seat, Beth the one in the middle, and Mark the one right
behind Jim and me. The station wagon didn't offer the com-
forts of home, but we shared some wonderful times talking,
singing, laughing, playing games, and seeing America when-
ever Jim needed to travel for business. We also spent our summer vacations during those early years traveling to various
spots in the U.S.

The kids were in high school when Jim and I started our
speaking engagements. We would check the children's activity calendars before scheduling an engagement to make sure
we wouldn't miss their significant activities. As much as we
traveled, we never missed one of Mark's high school basketball games.

Technically, it probably wouldn't have mattered if we had
spent three hours with Mark the day we left if we then missed
his basketball game. We might actually have spent more individual time with him; however, the game was important to
him, and thus to us also. Sometimes parents don't know what
is important to their children and inadvertently overlook attending something of great significance to the child.

Recently a woman confided that she felt her parents were
never interested in her life or in what was important to her.

When asked for specifics, the women responded, "Never once did they attend any of my school functions that other parents attended, from Brownie Scout programs in the first grade to school plays or athletic events in high school when I was a cheerleader." Yet I know her parents feel that they were always available to the children, provided for their needs, and gave them a proper upbringing. When confronted with her feelings, the parents were totally shocked. "But we never knew you wanted us to attend. We thought kids would be embarrassed if their parents came to any of their school activities."

What a shame—a lifetime of a child feeling that her activities were not important to the parents all the while the parents were doing what they thought the child wanted! Somewhere along the way they had never learned to communicate.

Jim always found out what was important to the kids, especially our son Mark. No matter what Mark did, Jim tried to involve himself in it, even if Jim had no aptitude or abilities in that area.

"The greatest times we had together were when you or Dad put yourselves in my world, becoming totally involved with my life," my son Mark responded when I asked him to share with me some of his best memories of time spent together.

Children remember the times together and resent the times when they feel they were last on the parents' list of priorities. Love can't be bought. Families need time together for proper maintenance and growth. Nothing else can substitute for daily, personal interaction.

## • *Gifts* •

*W*hat shall we give our
   children?
Christmas is almost here.
Toys and games and playthings
As we do every year?

Yes, for the magic of toyland
Is part of the yuletide lore
To gladden the hearts of children
But we shall give something more.

We shall give them more patience
A more sympathetic ear,
A little more time for laughter
Or tenderly drying their tear.

We shall take time to teach them
The joy of doing some task.
We will try to find time to answer
More of the questions they ask.

Time to read books together
And take long walks in the sun.
Time for a bedtime story,
After the day is done.

We shall give these to our children
Weaving a closer tie,
Knitting our lives together
With gifts that money can't buy.

J. P. RICHARDSON

## • *The Gift's the Thing . . .* •

*P*eople protect their hearts by giving things instead of themselves. They readily give material gifts, but never give of themselves emotionally. It's too frightening to be so vulnerable. Many parents do this with their children. A number of my friends have told me that their parents never sat down with them to find out what they were like deep inside. Nor would their parents readily share about themselves. These friends had to judge their parents' love by the material things they were given, a poor substitute for true intimate love.

DICK PURNELL

## • *Teaching Responsibility* •

Few things help an individual more than to
place responsibility upon him, and to
let him know that you trust him.
BOOKER T. WASHINGTON

*I*f you want to teach your children to be responsible, give them responsibility. Sounds simple, and it is. The key, however, is to make them responsible for the consequences, as well as the action. All actions have consequences; all choices have consequences. Children need to learn to accept full responsibility for the consequences of their choices and actions. But too much responsibility too soon is just as bad as not enough responsibility for too long. Give responsibilities in accordance with each child's level of maturity, but always stretch their abilities; don't just give them things you know they can handle.

With responsibility comes independence. After kids handle their responsibilities successfully, it gives them the independence of being able to handle something on their own without their parents.

We tried to develop independence and responsibility very early in our children. They had a Social Security number and checking account by the time they were ten. Teaching financial responsibility starts at a very early age, probably around a year and a half, as soon as a child starts to see that pennies and nickles can be traded for candy or toys or put in a bank. Children need to learn to be responsible for taking care of their own possessions and find ways to earn money at a very early age. Two-year-old kids can pick up their own clothes or collect wastebaskets so Mom can empty them in the garbage can. Three–year–olds can empty the dishwasher or learn to wipe off the sink and counter with a sponge to keep it clean. Children need to accept full responsibility for the order and cleanliness of their possessions and living area. Also give them extra chores so they can earn money for the things they want.

Once we started our own business, our children started earning money after school by stuffing envelopes, filling packages, collating materials, or doing other chores. Most importantly, they learned the value of saving their money for something meaningful.

Our policy was to buy our children the essentials they needed, but they had to earn fifty percent of the money for any extras. This incentive not only taught them the value of work but they also learned how to find the best value for their money. When Mark wanted a sleeping bag for Boy Scouts he turned it into a real research project trying to determine what was the best value for his money—a cheap sleeping bag or a very expensive down sleeping bag.

In the sixth grade Katherine decided to save money for a car. Jim showed her how much it would cost and how much she would have to earn and how long it would take. Six years later she had enough money to pay cash for a car within her budget. Ten years later she is still using that car. Not only did she learn to postpone immediate gratification for something more important later, but she learned the thrill of paying for something with cash and not having to make payments on it plus interest.

Teaching children how to work and to love working is a valuable contribution parents can make to their lives. By the time the kids were older, our work involved traveling to seminars during the summer, where many participants also brought their own children. Our children designed a seminar themselves, and for more than ten years, they taught other kids how to set and reach goals, how to improve their self-esteem, and other concepts which many children don't learn. Both the kids who attended the seminar and our kids gained more confidence in themselves.

Travel has been a basic part of our lives since the kids were little. When we moved to Arizona from New Jersey, Jim gave Mark full responsibility for the map from Minnesota to Phoenix—deciding which route to take and telling Jim which turns to make. That's a lot of responsibility for a nine–year-old, but Jim never criticized a wrong decision and always praised Mark's good choices. When a tire blew out, Mark didn't play alongside the road or sit in the car; Jim showed him the process and made sure Mark could do it himself when the need arose. Taking advantage of "teachable moments" is important in developing responsibility.

As the kids grew older and our trips were on a tighter schedule, we started flying. The kids were often put in charge of the travel arrangements; they called the airlines, found the best prices, and arranged our departure and arrival times. A small matter, easily assigned to a travel agency, became a definite factor in teaching the kids to be responsible and independent.

Also, we taught our kids to pack their own suitcases when they were very young. They had to find out what the weather was like and what they would need. Most of all, they learned to live with the consequences of their actions.

When the kids were in grade school and junior high, we let them plan a family weekend fun trip of their choice. We allotted them $200 to cover all expenses for the trip and told them they could keep any money left over. You can't imagine what enthusiastic and skilled travel agents they became. They researched and analyzed the costs of the gas and oil, motel, various restaurants in the area, and incidental expenses. Jim and I left the decisions totally up to them and we had no idea where we were going or how until the day arrived! We had a great family weekend; they stayed within their budget and had $15 to spare.

Whatever your family priorities, each day affords many opportunities to teach children how to be responsible and independent citizens of the family and world. Don't overlook any opportunity to help develop and maintain the strength of each member of your family.

# • Responsibility •

CHILDREN VERY OFTEN are brought up believing they are guests in the home because they have nothing to do except live there.  G. BOWDEN HUNT

THE SUREST WAY to make it hard for your children is to make it soft for them.  WESLEYAN METHODIST

A CHILD WHO is allowed to be disrespectful to his parents will not have true respect for anyone.  BILLY GRAHAM

IF YOU WANT your children to keep their feet on the ground, put some responsibility on their shoulders.

UNKNOWN

BECOMING RESPONSIBLE ADULTS is no longer a matter of whether children hang up their pajamas or put dirty towels in the hamper, but whether they care about themselves and others—and whether they see everyday chores as related to how we treat this planet.  EDA LESHAN

THE CHILD WHO has everything done for him, everything given to him, and nothing required of him is a deprived child . . . . The parent who tries to please the child by giving in to him and expecting nothing from him ends up by pleasing no one, least of all the child. For in the end, when trouble results, the child will blame the parent for his gutlessness.

LARRY CHRISTENSON

THERE IS A danger of overprotecting children, a tendency that parents should guard against. Take hard work, for instance. The discipline of work is one of life's most important ones. Work requires certain adaptations, concentrations, and continuity of effort. Children have to learn how to work. It is a gradual process, a growing experience as a boy matures. As a young adult he's pretty liable to find the confinement of sticking to a task almost unbearable at times if he hasn't learned it earlier.

WALTER MACPEEK

# • *Healing the Hurts* •

*I* glanced out the kitchen window and saw the bright pink bicycle topple. And my five-year-old daughter Beth toppled with it.

I was sure she would soon be in for a kiss and a bandage so I went to the bathroom to rummage for some antiseptic. But both Beth and her bike were gone when I came back to the kitchen.

She must not have hurt herself, I thought. Leaning over the kitchen sink, I looked as far as possible down the street. Neither bike nor Beth were in sight.

I put the bandages on the counter. "She would have come in immediately if she was hurt," I reassured myself.

The box was eventually surrounded by empty glasses, pencil stubs, scraps of paper with notes—the usual paraphernalia of a busy Saturday afternoon when everybody was home.

Everybody that is, but Beth. At four o'clock I went to look for her. In the backyard behind the garage was a hump of grass, an old stump, and an ancient birdhouse. Beth often went back there to scatter bread for the birds. When I found her, she was sitting dejectedly on the grass, her left knee badly scraped.

"Beth! You hurt yourself! Why didn't you come in? That scrape needs some antiseptic."

A woebegone face looked up at me through a tangle of blond curls. Down her cheeks were smudge trails of undried tears.

Concerned and puzzled, I sat down next to her and held out my arms. "What's the matter, sweetheart? Doesn't your knee hurt?"

Her affirmative answer, muffled against my sweater, had an unsteady quaver in it.

I tilted her head back so I could have a clear look into those impossibly blue eyes. "Well, if it hurts, silly, why didn't you come in?" I gave her a tiny loving shake.

She answered me with the beginnings of a smile. "Antiseptic hurts worse, Mommie."

We laughed then, both of us. But I was reflective later. In one sense my little daughter's logic was impeccable. Antiseptics, curatives, therapies, surgery, in fact, almost anything having to do with the process of healing—those things do hurt. It hurts to be healed.

When the scrape is across our own souls, caused by a friend who betrays us, a parent who puts us down, a family member who causes us pain, a spouse who leaves us in the cold, the pain of healing is almost impossible to face. Rather than washing the wound and applying antiseptic, however, we often sit behind our emotional garages until someone discovers our pain. The only difference is someone will discover a child in pain. As adults we have to wash our own wounds and apply our own antiseptic of forgiveness.

# • Discipline as a Form of Love •

Our kids are the most valuable things we have. The causes
of delinquency are (1) lack of love; and (2) lack of
discipline. . . . Don't shortchange your children
for a ministry to a larger group. Don't
just help others . . . and let your
own kids go down the drain.

JIM VAUS

*W*hen Diane was a little girl, she loved to stand up in her high chair. Her father repeatedly told her to sit down, but she refused. Being an old-fashioned father he thought the only way to make her mind was to spank her. It didn't work. When he put her back in the high chair, she still stood up. He spanked her again. Back in the high chair she stood up again. Finally he forcibly bent her legs and fastened two belts around both her body and her legs so it was physically impossible for her to stand up. Was he teaching obedience? Hardly. When Diane realized she couldn't move and he had won the battle but not the war, she replied, "You just think I'm sitting down, I'm still standing up on the inside."

Unfortunately, many times discipline can cause outward compliance but inward rebellion at a very early age. My philosophy of discipline is simple and can be summed up in one word . . . PREVENTION.

Preventing discipline problems starts very early with choices you make as a couple and as a family. Choices about your values, choices about respect for authority, choices about the roles and responsibilities of each family member. Choices about how much time you spend with your family and how it is spent. Choices about how much you love your children and whether or not they are a higher priority than your work or other aspects of your life.

Obviously, children have different levels of curiosity, rebellion, and energy. What works with one child is not necessarily going to work with the others. However, your response to their actions can make a big difference to the child's behavior.

Recently Katherine told me about something she had done in seventh grade that I didn't know. She wasn't afraid then of how I might punish her; rather, the worst punishment possible for her was that I would be deeply disappointed in her. She loved me so much that she wanted to please me.

I believe that, if you establish authority with little children early and if they know you mean what you say, you can prevent discipline problems before they begin.

Failure to discipline is to tell your children you don't love them. Most frequently discipline problems are a cry for attention. Sometimes the only way children can get their parents' attention is by misbehaving or by getting in trouble with authorities.

Discipline is an important aspect of family life because it also teaches self-discipline. Without self-discipline your kids will never function as healthy adults.

# • *Discipline* •

DISCIPLINE IS DEMANDED of the athlete to win a game. Discipline is required for the captain running his ship. Discipline is needed for the pianist to practice for the concert. Only in the matter of personal conduct is the need for discipline questioned. But if parents believe standards are necessary, then discipline certainly is needed to attain them.

GLADYS BROOKS

CORRECTION AND DISCIPLINE are good for children. If a child has his own way, he will make his mother ashamed of him. . . . Discipline your son and you can always be proud of him.

PROVERBS

WE UNDERSTAND THE paradox of discipline and freedom—that you're not doing a child a service in giving him no limits. If you show him what the restrictions are, he will find ways to fly absolutely free within those limits.

NOEL STOOKEY

# • *Twelve Rules for Raising Delinquent Children* •

1. Begin with infancy to give the child everything he wants. In this way he will grow up to believe the world owes him a living.

2. When he picks up bad words, laugh at him. This will make him think he's cute. It will also encourage him to pick up "cuter" phrases that will blow off the top of your head later.

3. Never give him any spiritual training. Wait until he is twenty-one and then let him "decide for himself."

4. Avoid use of the word *wrong*. It may develop a guilt complex. This will condition him to believe later, when he is arrested for stealing a car, that society is against him and he is being persecuted.

5. Pick up everything he leaves lying around—books, shoes, and clothes. Do everything for him so that he will be experienced in throwing all responsibility on others.

6. Let him read any printed matter he can get his hands on. Be careful that the silverware and drinking glasses are sterilized, but let his mind feast on garbage.

7. Quarrel frequently in the presence of your children. In this way they will not be too shocked when the home is broken up later.

8. Give a child all the spending money he wants. Never let him earn his own. Why should he have things as tough as you had them?

9. Satisfy his every craving for food, drink, and comfort. See that every sensual desire is gratified. Denial may lead to harmful frustration.

10. Take his part against neighbors, teachers, policemen. They are all prejudiced against your child.

11. When he gets into real trouble, apologize for yourself by saying, "I never could do anything for him."

12. Prepare for a life of grief. You will be likely to have it.

*ECONOMIC INTELLIGENCE*

## • *Parent's Prayer* •

*T*hey are little only once, Lord. Grant me the wisdom and patience to teach them to follow in your footsteps and prepare them for what is to come.

They are little only once, Lord. Make me take the time to play pretend, to read or tell a story, to cuddle. Don't let me for one minute think anything is more important than the school play, the recital, the big game, fishing, or the quiet walk hand in hand. All too soon, Lord, they will grow away and there is no turning back. Let me have my memories with no regrets.

Please help me to be a good parent, Lord. When I must discipline, let me do it in love; let me be firm, but fair; let me correct and explain with patience.

They are growing away, Lord. While I have the chance, let me do my best for them. For the rest of our lives, please, Lord, let me be their very best friend.     MARY L. ROBBINS

# • *Companions* •

*L*ord,
sometimes I am frightened by the weight I feel
to bring up these children
that you have entrusted to me
because in our time,
full of confusion and potential,
it seems harder and harder
to know how to raise children.

I know that I will make mistakes,
that I will fail my children,
that my strength and patience will not be sufficient,
that I will make the wrong decisions,
and that at times my love will grow weak.

Around me I see parents
laboring under the same weight,
afraid in the same way,
trying their best,
reading, feeling, growing
to stay close to their children
so that they will have the best possible start.

Help us all to keep love going,
and put your blessing on our love
which then has a chance to overcome
all the mistakes we will make.
Help us to know what it means practically
to be real companions to our children.

ULRICH SCHAFFER
*LION PUBLISHING,* *1980*

# • *Going Beyond Acceptance* •

People have a way of becoming what you encourage
them to be—not what you nag them to be.
SCUDDER N. PARKER

*O*ne of the great benefits of being a mother and having a family is that the relationship is not one-sided. Motherhood is not all giving; it is give *and* take. As much as I give to my family, they always give back in equal or greater measure, and it never ceases to amaze me.

When I started my speaking career, my children were all in high school or college. They knew my fears and need for reassurance and growth in this area. Probably one of my most difficult speaking engagements was before the California Dental Association meeting in Anaheim in the early 1970s. I had a year and a half to worry, prepare my talk, fret over what to wear, and pray.

Ten minutes before the moment arrived, however, I began to perspire profusely and not a single word would come out of my parched mouth. Frantically I hid in the last cubicle of the women's restroom and in vain tried to control my shaking knees and get a grip on myself. Then the countdown began. Ten, nine, eight, seven, six, five minutes and I still wasn't any better. Things were getting worse. Four, three, two, one and I was unable to get out of the restroom cubicle.

Then I realized the meeting would go on without me. No one would even miss me. Someone would take my place. I could choose between passing on one of the greatest opportunities of my professional career up to this point and spending the next hour degrading myself in the women's restroom. Isn't it amazing to reflect on how our choices are made? That still, small voice inside that says, "Just do it one more time."

Two minutes later I walked up and stood behind the podium facing a huge auditorium full of people. Before I could say a word, my eyes fell on a handwritten note that said, "Dear Mom, We love you and are so proud of you. We'll be praying for you every minute." Unbeknownst to me, our three children had come to hear me speak and offer their support and encouragement when I needed it the most. The large audience was no longer my concern. I couldn't disappoint our three children who were counting on me to do my best.

Acceptance recognizes persons as they now are. Encouragement celebrates what they may yet become with God's help.
ANONYMOUS

## • *Accepting the Unacceptable* •

*A*cceptance is the answer to all my problems today. When I am disturbed, it is because I find some person, place, thing, or situation—some fact of my life—unacceptable to me and I can find no serenity until I accept that person, place, thing, or situation as being exactly the way it is supposed to be at this moment. Nothing, absolutely nothing, happens in God's world by mistake; unless I accept life completely on life's terms, I cannot be happy. I need to concentrate not so much on what needs to be changed in the world as on what needs to be changed in me and in my attitudes. Only then do I have the power to influence change in my world.
UNKNOWN

# PART FOUR

# Surviving the Storms

# • *When Trouble Comes* •

Your family is what you've got . . . . It's your limits and your possibilities. Sometimes you'll get so far away from it you'll think you're outside its influence forever; then before you figure out what's happening, it will be right beside you, pulling the strings. Some people get crushed by their families. Others are saved by them.

PETER COLLIER

*C*onflicts come in all families. Situations and people change. Things we count on don't materialize and people we trust let us down.

Divorce, emotional or physical abandonment, leaving home, coming back, death—all take their toll on the family unit. The "if onlys" start. If only they had done things differently . . . or if only alcohol hadn't been encouraged at home . . . or if only father or mother hadn't worked all the time . . .

What went wrong? Who's to blame? What do we do now?

Surviving the storms that come our way will be the greatest test of the strength of the family ties. Can you forgive and start over? Can you trust? Now more than ever before, absolute truth is required. Family ties once tested or even severed with hatred and resentment can be rebuilt with love and forgiveness. Broken families can be put back together, but probably the new one will be different from the original.

Families are full of flawed people. We are all flawed, but that doesn't mean the family needs to be destroyed. Our survival comes when we adapt to meet the needs of the new family situation.

The family is crucial to the future of our youth and society. We must learn tolerance and flexibility. God has joined you together. Your family is family forever.

# • *Conflict* •

IN THE ALL-IMPORTANT world of family relations, three words are almost as powerful as the famous "I love you." They are "Maybe you're right."    OREN ARNOLD

MORE THAN TIME is required to heal a badly broken family. It takes meaningful actions and knowing how to say "I love you."    GRAHAM KERR

YOUTH CAN MEASURE in only one direction—from things as they are forward to their ideal of what things ought to be. They cannot measure backward, to things as they used to be, because they have not lived long enough, and they cannot measure laterally, to the condition of other societies on this earth, because they have not yet had the opportunity to know them well. Older people must add these two measurements. This is the core reason why the generation gap exists and why it will always exist.    ERIC SEVAREID

# • *Golden Rules for Living* •

1. If you open it, close it.
2. If you turn it on, turn it off.
3. If you unlock it, lock it up.
4. If you break it, admit it.
5. If you can't fix it, call in someone who can.
6. If you borrow it, return it.
7. If you value it, take care of it.
8. If you make a mess, clean it up.
9. If you move it, put it back.
10. If it belongs to someone else, get permission to use it.
11. If you don't know how to operate it, leave it alone.
12. If it's none of your business, don't ask questions.

UNKNOWN

# • *Prayer of St. Francis of Assisi* •

*L*ord, make me an instrument of Thy peace;
where there is hatred, let me sow love;
where there is injury, pardon;
where there is doubt, faith;
where there is despair, hope;
where there is darkness, light;
and where there is sadness, joy.

O Divine Master, grant that
I may not so much seek
to be consoled as to console;
to be understood as to understand;
to be loved, as to love;
for it is in giving that we receive,
it is in pardoning that we are pardoned
and it is in dying that we are born to eternal life.

# • *Giving a Child Freedom* •

TRUE PARENTHOOD IS self-destructive. The wise parent is one who effectively does himself out of his job as parent. The silver cord must be broken. It must not be broken too abruptly, but it must be broken. The child must cease to be a child. . . . The wise parent delivers his child over to society.

ROBERT HOLMES

CHILDREN HAVE NOT grown up until they can look at their parents as real people. Little children see their parents as paragons. Mother is the most beautiful woman in the world; father, the strongest man. Then comes the stage when everything is wrong with the parents. Maturity is being able to deal with parents as human beings; neither perfect nor impossible, but loved.

GEORGE SWEAZEY

HOLD EVERYTHING IN your hands lightly—otherwise it hurts when God pries your fingers open.

CORRIE TEN BOOM

# • *When Your Child Grows Up* •

*O*h, never hold a loved one clenched so tight
And carefully within protective hands
That like a frightened bird he takes his flight
Into a gentler and more sunny land.

Have faith that as you freely let him dare
His wings to seek the outposts of the sky
That he will send his love across the air,
More "yours" than some tame bird that cannot fly.

For what you hold you lose, and learn to weep;
But what your heart sets free you always keep.

JEAN HOGAN DUDLEY

# • *Learn from the Eagles* •

As an eagle stirs up its nest, Hovers over its young,
Spreading out its wings, taking them up,
carrying them on its wings . . .
DEUTERONOMY 32:11

*M*other eagles have a delightful way of getting their young to fly. Rather than allowing them to remain in the comfort of their nest, the mother gradually pushes out all the fuzz and moss that makes the nest comfortable and starts turning the twigs and feathers up on end so the nest becomes uncomfortable.

If that doesn't entice the baby eagles to try out their wings, she gradually pushes the young ones out of the nest. Rather than allow them to panic or crash on the rocks below, the mother eagle swoops down and catches them on her wings. Over and over the process is repeated until each young eagle learns to fly on its own.

Like young eagles, children are meant to leave the nest and fly. This is a gradual process, allowing them to venture out on their own, offering them assistance when it is needed, and then returning to the nest. All through childhood a family's little eagles are encouraged to stretch their wings, but come home for rest.

There comes a day, however, when children should venture out and start building their own nests. Whether it is leaving for college, career, marriage, or just seeing the world, parents must make the transition by giving them the desire to fly, not by making the nest more comfortable. Remember the eagle: let your children leave the nest. Parents are not for leaning on, but to make leaning unnecessary.

# • *Flight Clearance* •

*W*ait! Don't go.
You've been here such a little while
So much we haven't done
I haven't said.
Don't go, my child.

I watched you.
Damp curls, clutching Teddy's foot
In slumber you lay—angelic.
I wept—prophetic
Of future cares, my child.

I turned around
You filled the bed, arms flung wide
Wings awaiting take-off.
Please don't ask
For flight clearance, my child.

How short a time since
I bore you in womb, in arms, in heart.
My labor pains return
Each time you plunge
Head-first into the world, my child.

You've come to go
From my lap, my knees, my side
But never from my love.
Like Abraham with Isaac
I give you up—I receive you again.

Forever, my child.

VICKI HUFFMAN

# • *Letter from College* •

*M*other,

The funniest thing is happening to me. I feel like everything in my world is changing. What do I do? I don't know whether it's good or bad, but it's scary. Beth's getting married, and I feel like I'm losing her. You and Dad are the same, your life is stable and I feel like I'm not affecting it in any way. Your life goes on without me just fine.

I don't think I want to be on my own. I like the security of my family of five and dog Adam!! I don't care about growing up; I just want to be a chubby kid on Calle Redonda the rest of my life, going to Hawaii every summer with my buddies Mark and Beth, and then coming home to live in the same house forever. You can cook, and Beth and I will trade off nights doing the dishes. You can even travel some because Gramma will come over from Lindstrom Gardens and stay with us. We'll play Scrabble and eat goulash casserole. See what I mean?

My problem is that's impossible and I don't think coming home at Thanksgiving is going to make it better.

Well, I'm going to bed now. Remember cause I'm your relative! And I love you!

KATHERINE (YOUR HOMESICK GIRL)

*(Obviously, a sense of humor amidst hard times helps!)*

# • *Attachment and Release* •

$\mathcal{T}$he love which grows into a lasting marriage needs both attachment and release. After the partners learn to be close, to be companions, and to care for each other, release is an expression of trust, respect, and acceptance. Can the partners allow each other freedom to grow as individuals? A man who delights in his wife's separate blooming will find her more closely his own because he released her. The woman who encourages her husband's personal fulfillment will sense his gratitude and satisfaction. If one partner is afraid to let go and tries to control the growth and creativity of the other, love will be strangled.    ROBERT O. BLOOD, *MARRIAGE*

# • *Broken Dreams* •

*A*s children bring their broken
   toys
With tears for us to mend,
I brought my broken dreams to God
Because He was my Friend.

But then instead of leaving Him
In peace to work alone,
I hung around and tried to help
With ways that were my own.

At last I snatched them back and cried,
"How could You be so slow"—
"My child," He said,
"What could I do?
You never did let go."

AUTHOR UNKNOWN

## • *Letting Go* •

$\mathcal{I}$ see children as kites. You spend a lifetime trying to get them off the ground. You run with them until you're both breathless. They cross, then hit the rooftop. You patch and comfort, adjust and teach. You watch them lift up by the wind and assure them that someday they will fly and finally, finally they are airborne.

They need more strength and they keep letting out, but with each twist of the ball of twine there's a sadness that goes with joy. The kite becomes more distant and you know it won't be long before that beautiful creature will snap the life-line that binds you together and will soar as it is meant to soar and be free and alone. Only then do you know that you did your job. ERMA BOMBECK

## • *Can Your Family Say This about You?* •

$\mathcal{F}$or the freedom to be as I am . . . for the inspiration to be more . . . for the confidence that I can do much, for the re-newed desire to reach my potential . . . for the willingness to acknowledge my needs . . . for the greater awareness of the needs and potentials of others . . . for all that you have meant to me . . . I am grateful. ELLEN EWRLANGER

# • *The Collapse of a Family* •

ONE OF THE great concerns of today is the collapse of the family as a meaningful unit in our society. It is said that the average person in the U.S.A. spends seventy-six percent of his lifetime at home. Yet our homes are too often split-level traps from which we want to flee. So often, each member of a family goes his separate way. Consequently, our family relationships are fractured, or frozen at best. We do not know each other. What is worse, many do not care.

WILLIAM ENRIGHT

ROBERT FROST DEFINED a home as a place where, when you come there, they have to take you in. Many people are beginning to doubt that. For too many Americans, home has become a place where the family may convene on major holidays, with just about the same kind of conviviality and the same masks to hide real feelings as one sees at business and professional conventions.

DUSTY SKLAR

## • *Surviving a Broken Family* •

$\mathscr{A}$ sixteen-year-old girl shared with me an essay she wrote for an English class. The assignment was to write about a person either living or dead. . . .

### THIS MAN

This man has changed my life. This man has taught me what I want out of life and what I don't want. This man showed me right from wrong while helping me form my own opinions, values, and ideals. This man has no idea of the sort of impact he has had on my life. This man is not alive. This man is not dead. This man is my father.

As I think back over my childhood he was never there to turn to for love, understanding, or even a hug. His cold-hearted attitude hurt, for I didn't know why he treated me as if I were nonexistent. In every attempt I made to make contact with him, I was turned away only to become more confused and hurt, not able to understand why a little girl's daddy did not want to see her. An obvious difference became apparent to me between my family and that of others as I saw the warmth and concern my friends' fathers showed them. I reveled in any extra attention given to me by these fathers and acquired a special love and admiration for them. The feeling of acceptance by a father was irreplaceable since it proved that I was not incapable of being loved as a daughter and it was possible that the problem existed within my father and not within me.

This man has not shown pride in my accomplishments nor has he denied credit for them. This man has not encouraged me. This man has acted as if he could care less one way or the other about me. This man has not been involved in my life. This man is not dead. This man is not alive. This man is my father.

Without his help and without his guidance, I have had academic success, I have formed high morals, and have developed strong personality qualities which will take me far. His lack of interest in my future goals and aspirations has done nothing to restrain me. If anything, it has motivated me to show him up and prove that I can accomplish anything and I don't need his support to do it. Without him there for my first date and without him there for my first heartbreak, I still proudly survived. I learned to stand tall and set my sights high and not lower my standards, values, or morals for anyone. Without him I learned to remain firm in my faith and stick up for what I believe in. I learned what I want for my own children and what I don't want for them. Through his absent teaching, by negation, I have learned more from this man than anyone else I know.

This man has taught me how to laugh, love, and respect. This man has taught me the importance of friendships and the meaning of happiness. And most importantly he has taught me how to forgive. This man is not alive. This man is not dead. This man is my father . . . and I love him.

NATALIE ESTRUTH*

---

*Laurene Johnson and Georglyn Rosenfeld, *Divorced Kids* (Nashville: Thomas Nelson, 1990), 216–217.

## • *Families Are Forever* •

*F*amilies are forever,
They never seem to bend
A timeless bond of love and hope
On which we all depend.

They provide a place to which we flee
When the world grows cold and dreary
To be secure and find a hug
When we have grown too weary.

To build us up when we are scared
And help us bear the pain
Then give us strength to stand alone
And venture out again.

As many problems come our way
Apart we may sometimes drift
With each other we need to strive
To close the growing rift.

With this knowledge we will be strong
Should death or divorce attack
And please love us unconditionally
Cause we're hungry to love you back.

A family is like a rainbow
Made up of different members
And unless each works together
It will fade like a fire's embers.

The colors of the rainbow
Represent many special things
That we often long to share with you
Our hopes, our fears, our dreams.

The yellow stands for happiness
That warms us deep inside
The blue is there in all our sorrow
That we may try to hide.

The gray is death and bitter endings
That wrench our tender souls
But green brings new growth to take their place
And once more make us whole.

Family ties provide unending strength
Just like rainbow colors from above
And through time, support and caring
Families become rich and radiant with love.

Though stars may shine for many years
And worlds may come and go
Though skies go on for miles and miles
Not one of them can show,

The strength that families do contain
And troubles that they can weather
For each of these will eventually end
But families will go on forever.

So to our parents, we make this plea:
Support us in our endeavors
Create a stronger bond of love
And make families last forever.

> THE YOUTH OF THE NATIONAL SPEAKERS
> ASSOCIATION 1988 CONVENTION,
> PHOENIX, ARIZONA

## • *The Paradox of Forgiveness* •

. . . IT LOOKS CONTRADICTORY to our self-interest to let go of wrongs, but most of those who hurt us are people we are closest to—parents, siblings, spouses, friends. Trying to get even only leads to a vicious circle of retaliation. In the long run, forgiveness is the best choice for the forgiver—and the forgiven.                                             DONALD HOPE

FORGIVENESS IS THE oil that lubricates the friction of closeness in the daily routine of the home.          JOHN HOWELL

HATRED CAN BE an acid that does more damage to the vessel in which it is stored than to the object on which it's poured.                                                          UNKNOWN

BY TAKING REVENGE a man is but even with his enemy, but in passing it over, he is superior.                   UNKNOWN

WHAT'S THE USE of being forgiven if I have to promise not to do it again?                                  ASHLEY BRILLIANT

A GOOD MEMORY is fine, but the ability to forgive and forget is the true test of greatness.                     UNKNOWN

WRITE THE WRONGS that are done to you in sand, but write the good things that happen to you on a piece of marble. Let go of all emotions such as resentment and retaliation, which diminish you, and hold onto the emotions, such as gratitude and joy, which increase you.                    ARABIC PROVERB

A TRUE APOLOGY is more than just acknowledgement of a mistake. It is recognition that something you have said or done has damaged a relationship and that you care enough about the relationship to want it repaired and restored.

NORMAN VINCENT PEALE

FOR ME TO fail to forgive myself or anyone else who has offended me is to imply that I have a higher standard of forgiveness than God, because whatever it is that has so hurt me that I can't forgive it, God already has.      HAL LINDSAY

NEVER DOES A man stand so tall as when he foregoes revenge, and dares to forgive an injury.      J. HAROLD SMITH

TO KNOW ALL is to forgive all.      ANCIENT PROVERB

THE MOST IMPORTANT ingredient in forgiveness is love. At its best, forgiveness is done for the very sake of those who have trespassed against us. Then we see forgiveness at its most powerful—renewing friendships, marriages, and careers.

Forgiveness works best when the hurt person has had time to face his anger, to recognize his own contributions to the debacle and to realize the consequences of a refusal to forgive.

THOMAS FLEMING

## • *Forgiveness Is the Key to Happiness* •

*S*ometimes, we are tempted to feel like a victim and want to find someone to blame. Yet, that seldom eases our pain. Forgiveness can be our key to seeing the world differently.

Forgiveness is letting go of the past. It is letting go of whatever we think other people, the world, or God has done to us or whatever we think we did to them.

Forgiveness is celestial amnesia; that is, letting go of all the memories of the past except the love we have given and received.

Through forgiveness, we can stop the endless cycle of pain and guilt and look upon ourselves and others with love.

Forgive now. Don't wait.                                    UNKNOWN

# • *Blooming Again* •

*C*hildren grow up, leave home, move away, and don't come home too often. Sometimes the parents suffer from the empty-nest syndrome, feeling useless and unwanted. Frequently they challenge their own marriage relationship and wonder what keeps them together now. Ironically, many parents stay together until the kids graduate from high school "for the sake of the children." Yet statistics now show that when parents divorce after the children leave home, it is more difficult for those children to adjust to the divorce than for those whose parents divorced during their growing-up years. The young adults begin to question the validity of all relationships and have a difficult time becoming involved in any meaningful relationships themselves.

If your family now seems obsolete, you can find new meaning and beauty in your relationship. Work on those dreams you set aside because the family's needs came first. Maybe now is the time to go back to school, change careers, travel, sell your home, or paint your own rainbow.

For Jim and me, our lives have taken on new meaning since the children are gone. We moved into a home more suitable for our business and entertaining needs, one that has a guest house for Jim's mother and stepfather, Agnes and Bob, whom we adore. Our schedule now involves ten times more travel and because our children are grown, they no longer require our consistent presence at home. When our children do visit with their families, we have a wonderful time of jubilee and rejoicing; but our lives are not barren just because they are gone. Instead, we are now freer to work on our own self-fulfillment, which, ultimately, deeply affects them.

If your kids are gone—and maybe even your spouse is gone—that doesn't mean you are useless. Families aren't just blood relatives. Find someone who needs you. Be a family to that person or persons. Young people away from home or children of divorce frequently could use a part-time mom or dad. Friends your own age need a brother or sister. Be an aunt or uncle or grandma or grandpa to lonely hearts you see on your life's journey.

Life is full of tragedy, but you can plant flowers where weeds once grew. Don't wait for others to bring you flowers; fill your life and soul with flowers. Reach out to others.

## • *Building on Today* •

After a while you learn the subtle difference between holding a hand and chaining a soul. And you learn that love doesn't mean leaning, and company doesn't mean security. And you begin to learn that kisses aren't contracts, and presents aren't promises. And you begin to accept your defeats with your head up and your eyes open, with the grace of an adult, not the grief of a child. And you learn to build all your roads on today, because tomorrow's ground is too uncertain for plans.

After a while you learn that even sunshine burns if you get too much. So plant your own garden and decorate your own soul, instead of waiting for someone to bring you flowers. And you learn that you really can endure, that you really are strong, and you really do have worth.          UNKNOWN

# PART FIVE

# *The*
# *Gift*
# *of*
# *Family*

. . . . . . . . . . . . . . . . . . . .

# · New Generations ·

A family is a link to the past, a bridge to the future.
ALEX HALEY

Some family relationships have precarious beginnings. Do you have any family relationships that were difficult from the very start? Most families do. Frequently it occurs when you receive a whole new set of relatives through marriage.

When I married Jim, our relationship did not come with a ready-made link from me to my mother-in-law, Agnes. She didn't fit any stereotype or preconceived idea I had of what a mother should be. My own mother was a stay-at-home homemaker. She loved to make soup and bread. Agnes loved to read books and work crossword puzzles and teach school.

My relationship with Jim's mom was pretty much limited to honoring her as the mother of the man I loved and with whom I intended to spend the rest of my life. I honored her by showing her respect and esteem, but I didn't really consider her a mother to me.

Aware of my distance from Agnes, my mother gave me some invaluable advice on the day she died. Somehow she must have known it was going to be her last day on this earth. I will never forget her words, the soft, kind admonition she spoke only moments before she died.

"You've been a wonderful daughter to me," she exhorted. "Now choose to become the same kind of daughter to your *other* mother—Jim's mother. She is a wonderful woman. Decide to love her and call her 'Mother.'"

I wanted to honor my mother's wish, but to overcome the habits of the first years of my marriage and to initiate and call Agnes 'Mother' was very difficult.

I was devastated by my mother's death, and Agnes came to my rescue. She opened her arms and her heart to my sorrow and came to spend that first summer after Mother's death with me. I'll never forget the day I first called her Mother—heart pounding and still unsure I truly wanted to. She responded wonderfully—openly and, yes, as is her style, very pragmatically. My mother never knew it, but by encouraging me to transfer some of my love for her to Agnes, she facilitated one of my closest relationships.

Time passes quickly and soon it was my turn to have "children-in-law." I was faced with the challenges of accepting and loving these special people—Melody, Curt, and Ken—when they were not the "stereotype" children Jim and I had raised: They were wonderful, but different. Obviously, bonding isn't instant. This is a process, a process of give and take as we build a strong bond of acceptance and love.

## • *Learning to Love and Forgive* •

*D*ear Naomi—

Thank you so much for giving me the loving gift of two whole days of being your friend! . . . I can't juggle the different components in my mind to measure or sort what the greatest gift of all was. Certainly time was a tremendous gift; I value so much the time you gave me. Thank you. I feel rich!

Attention—I felt listened to, interacted with, attended to, by you, and it was like sitting in a jacuzzi—warm all over, invigorating, refreshing, soothing, healing—that is the most wonderful experience! Just feeling it from you inspires me to want my clients to experience that in therapy. Attending to another person is a powerful therapeutic intervention . . . and I think it is also an art . . . and a gift of love. Thank you for that gift.

Thank you for trusting me. I felt like you did. I felt like you shared with me new little glimpses of who you are—how you feel—what matters to you—how you think and care and experience others. Those glimpses and the trust that goes with them are precious to me. Thank you . . . Thanks for sharing your taste with me and expanding mine as we shopped together. Thank you for giving me new thoughts about forgiveness—sharpening—filling in the picture. . . . Please keep in dialogue with me on this as much as you want to. I have so much to learn from you about forgiveness, in theory and in practice. . . . Thank you for sharing you and your world with me. . . .

Thank you for your love. I love you. . . .          MELODY

# • *Thy People Shall Be My People* •

The . . . faith that is in you . . . dwelt first in your
grandmother Lois and your mother Eunice.
2 TIMOTHY 1:5

*I* have always been fascinated by the Bible story of Ruth and
her mother-in-law Naomi. After Ruth's husband died, she
had to decide whether to stay in her own country with her
sister-in-law Orpah, or go to the country of Judah with
Naomi. Ruth decided to go with her mother-in-law, although
Naomi urged her to stay. Ruth's response of love to Naomi is
recorded in the following words and frequently used as part of
marriage ceremonies:

> Entreat me not to leave you, / Or to turn back from follow-
> ing after you; / For wherever you go, I will go; / And wher-
> ever you lodge, I will lodge; / Your people shall be my
> people, / And your God, my God. / Where you die, I will
> die, / And there will I be buried. / The LORD do so to me,
> and more also, / If anything but death parts you and me.
>
> RUTH 1:16–17

Later, Ruth married Boaz and had a son named Obed.
Naomi became the child's nurse and raised it as though he
were her own son. Friends who knew the two women told
Naomi her daughter-in-law Ruth was better to her than seven
sons could be. And Obed grew up to become the father of
Jesse, who was the father of David. What a wonderful heritage of love these two women shared together!

Are you building a heritage for those who follow you? Are
your children and grandchildren, nieces and nephews, aunts
and uncles going to have supportive relatives and friends to
ease their journey through life? Extended families are a wonderful gift to give to your children. Are you looking after only
your blood relatives, or are you also allowing your in-laws and
their families to share your heritage?

# • *Sharing Our Memories* •

Each day comes just once in a lifetime—today you are
creating tomorrow's memories. Invest in positive
memories, for childhood memories mold
the person of the future.

MARION STROUD

*I* hope you and your family look back on your times together with fond memories. I hope that every day you are
making memories together, not only for yourself, but for future generations. Share your memories with younger generations, for your past is part of their identity.

Some of my earliest memories are of a little house in Fargo,
North Dakota. In the basement, Dad had a little den and a
craft shop filled with Indian artifacts and scouting memora-
bilia. Every night he would go down there and whittle. I
would alternate between watching him and watching Mother
work in the kitchen. At the close of every day we would come
together as a family for devotions.

During the summer we lived at a Boy Scout camp where
my dad was the camp director. Regardless of how busy he
was, each evening after the campers were all in their tents we
gathered as a family to sing, tell stories, or pray around our
own private campfire. My parents always pulled away from
the demands of others to give the most and best attention to
their family.

Although my children did not get to know their maternal
grandparents, I have shared many memories of my parents
with my kids. I hope you do the same with your children.
They may not yet appreciate it, but they will some day. Your
job isn't to make them appreciate memories. Your job is to
preserve those memories in some form so they can be shared
with future generations.

# • Picturing Our Memories •

*P*ictures are memories, recording events and people, celebrations and growth.

Are your family pictures in various boxes and drawers throughout your house, attic, and garage so that it takes hours to find a particular picture you want to show someone? If you can't manage the fun of placing them in photo albums, at least put them in a central location where it is easier for others to find and enjoy them.

Over the years I have filled many photo albums with pictures of our family. When our children come home they frequently get out the picture books and sit for hours, giggling and laughing over some of the pictures. Although taking and organizing the pictures is a memory gift to my children and their children, I myself was recently blessed in a special way.

Around the time of my fiftieth birthday, I was speaking in Minnesota, where we had lived when I was twenty-three. Seventy-eight friends I have known during our years there, as well as friends and business associates from eight different states, surprised me with a party.

Unbeknownst to me, a few months prior to my birthday, Katherine and Ken had gone through our photo albums and lovingly selected pictures which represented my life story. They put the pictures in order and transformed them into a video, with the songs significant in my life at each time. It's a special gift for me to realize that our children knew me well enough to take out the right pictures and to accompany them with the right music to represent my life and my spiritual faith.

Pictures are a wonderful gift of memories. Healthy families find creative ways to recycle memories through the gift of pictures. I heard about a woman whose most cherished Christmas tree ornament was one her son made for her in the first grade with his picture on it. After her kids were grown, her daughter created thirty-six different Christmas ornaments, each one containing a photo of each year of their childhood. What a precious gift!

My friend's mother worked many weeks going through their unorganized family pictures to create a surprise photo album for each of their children after they were grown and married. Her gift of remembrance included a sampling of photos from each year of their life, including homes in which they lived, schools they attended, and favorite friends.

Another woman created a birthday album for each of her children. It lovingly documented birthday activities for each year of her children's lives.

In many of our family pictures Beth and Katherine are holding hands. Katherine gave her sister Beth a precious photo album consisting of pictures of the two of them holding hands at various stages in their lives.

Are you taking full advantage of photographs which capture brief moments in your family's life? Look for opportunities to give the gift of yourself—create a unique book of picture memories for someone in your family.

## • *Making Life Worthwhile* •

$\mathcal{C}$ommenting on her numerous interviews with people just before they died, Elizabeth Kübler Ross said,

> Not one of them has ever told me how many houses she had or how many handbags or sable coats. What they tell you are very tiny, almost insignificant moments of their lives— where they went fishing with a child, or they tell of the mountain-climbing trips to Switzerland. Some brief moments in an interpersonal relationship. These are the things that keep people going to the end. . . . They remember little moments that they had long forgotten, and they suddenly have a smile on their faces. And they begin to reminisce about little memories that make their whole life meaningful and worthwhile.

# • *A House and a Home* •

*W*hat is the difference between a home and a house? Anybody can build a house; we need something more for the creation of a home. A house is an accumulation of brick and stone, with an assorted collection of manufactured goods; a home is the abiding place of ardent affection, of fervent hope, of genial trust.

There is many a homeless man who lives in a richly furnished house. There is many a modest house in the crowded street which is an illuminated and beautiful home. The sumptuously furnished house may be only an exquisitely sculptured tomb; the scantily furnished house may be the very hearthstone of the eternal God.

The Bible does not say very much about homes; it says a great deal about the things that make them.

It speaks about life and love and joy and peace and rest! If we get a house and put these into it, we shall have secured a home.  JOHN HENRY JOWETT,* *THE MARRIAGE AFFAIR*

---

*J. Allan Petersen, *The Marriage Affair* (Wheaton, IL: Tyndale House, 1971).

# • *Unlocking Our Memories* •

*In* later life, when we have reached the introspective age and are prone to live in memories rather than in hopes and anticipations, association adds its mystic spell to the charm and potency of certain strains of music. The half-forgotten fragment of a line, heard or recalled by accident, is fraught with recollections sadly sweet, like flowers from the grave of dead joys. It will unlock storehouses of memory.

ROBERT LOVE TAYLOR

# • *It's a Boy* •
. . . . . . . . . . . . . .

*T*he gift of family, a legacy of love. The legacy goes on and on—as we rejoice together over the birth of the grandchildren, who will someday have their own children, and as we introduce any member of the family into the family of God.

My mother was present when I received this eternal heritage. As a young girl, I discovered the truth of 1 John 5:11—"God has given us eternal life, and this life is in His Son"—and I committed my life to Christ. On that significant and tender day, I prayed with my mother and committed to begin a new life as a child of God, claiming the words of John 1:12: "But as many as received Him, to them He gave the right to become children of God, even to those who believe in His name."

Not only did I receive the gift of everlasting life that day, but I became a part of the eternal family of God, the greatest family of all. And I received a legacy from the Greatest Love of All that I have passed on to my children and now pass on to my grandchildren.

We have been blessed with the birth of five grandsons in the last three years. While anticipating the birth of the fifth grandson (Beth and Curt's third son) I promised Beth I would be with her in the delivery room if at all possible, as I had been for her first and Katherine's first.

A few days before the baby was due, I was scheduled to speak at a seminar in Eugene, Oregon, before five hundred people. The seminar had been planned for more than a year and I needed to keep the obligation. The night before we spoke, Beth told me she might be delivering early. I assured her I would hurry to California the next afternoon after I had finished speaking.

That morning as I spoke, I shared with my audience that a definition of a professional was someone who does even better when they don't feel like it and that my heart was really with Beth that day, but I would be even better because of my commitment to them.

As I came to the end of the first hour-and-a-half session I repeated a story I often tell about the first baby's heart transplant at Loma Linda Hospital. A couple in Michigan had a baby who was dying and had agreed to donate the heart of the infant to a child at Loma Linda after their child's death.

My husband and I happened to visit the hospital on the day the baby was scheduled for surgery. While we were there, we caught the buzz of a rumor through the hospital that the helicopter had just arrived with the heart of the donor. The air was electric with the staff's excitement.

A week later, I noticed a photograph of the donor family in *Time* magazine. The magazine contained an interview, in which the mother of the infant donor had gone in to say good-bye to her child. "She rubbed his arms and said, 'Now you do a very good job,' and he did."

Each time I tell the story I offer the challenge to the audience that that child had only a very few days to live on this earth. We have had many more. Each morning, we have to look at ourselves in the mirror and ask if we have done a very good job with the days that have been given to us.

I closed the session with a poem and the audience burst into applause.

Suddenly, the audience of five hundred were not only clapping but gasping and crying. Confused, I noticed the people pointing to the overhead projector screen behind me. I turned around and read

IT'S A BOY
QUINLAN JEFFREY HAMANN
6 lbs. 5 oz.
Score:
Grandsons—5
Granddaughters—0

I wept; the audience wept. The applause continued. The tears and applause were for new life, new hope; for me, there is one more generation to receive the legacy of love.